W9-AYJ-361

VOYAGES

Exploring the Art of Greg Mort

with essays by the artist

SEA GLASS PUBLISHING

First Printing

Published by Sea Glass Publishing
PO Box 156 – Chestertown, Maryland 21620 U.S.A.

Editor: Thomas Y. Canby
Design: Sara Birkemeier and George Scott, 8 DOT Graphics

www.seaglasspublishing.com
www.gregmort.com

VOYAGES – Exploring the Art of Greg Mort
Printed in China
Library of Congress Control Number 2007925739
ISBN 978-0-9753246-7-7

Key to the Stars
watercolor
19" x 25" . 1995
Collection of Gerald and Kristin Strid

To Nadine, Kamissa and Jonathan who have inspired and enriched my voyage.

"For small creatures such as we
the vastness is bearable only through love."

FROM THE BOOK *CONTACT* BY CARL SAGAN

Acknowledgements

My sincere thanks must first go to the brilliant and insightful Nancy and Richard LaMotte and their staff at Sea Glass Publishing, including Devon DeMeritt and Kay MacIntosh. Their talents, along with those of 8 Dot Graphic Designers Sara Birkemeier and George Scott have produced a fine-art book that is in itself a work of art. I am greatly indebted to multifaceted author and editor Tom Canby, who helped me express my feelings and experiences more clearly and effectively.

I am sincerely indebted to Francesco Bertola for his inspirational reflections and creative energy. Interviews with writer and editor J. Kelly Beatty helped me explore my artistic life from perspectives I had never considered. My deep appreciation also goes to Ambassador Cynthia P. Schneider for contributing her expertise as a renowned cultural art historian, scholar and author. I am humbled to count American literary icon Esmeralda Santiago as a fellow traveler on my creative sojourn and appreciate the generous contributions she and gifted poets Ellen Bishop, Jean Diemert, Heather Doyle and Anthony Petrosky have made by reflecting my images and emotions so artfully in their mesmerizing words.

An artist's relationship with his gallery is much like a marriage. I have been fortunate to forge true love affairs with both the Carla Massoni Gallery in Chestertown, Maryland, and the Somerville Manning Gallery in Greenville, Delaware. Carla Massoni, a respected authority and passionate visionary in the art world, has nurtured my artistic development in a manner that cannot be measured by manmade rules. This book project has been greatly enriched by Vickie Manning's creativity and endless hours of discussion, guidance and thoughtful advice. Sadie Somerville's sensitive but straightforward contributions have been invaluable, too. She provides balance and grace to all that surrounds her.

I am grateful to the many patrons who have provided encouragement and allowed special access to their collections for paintings that span my entire career, especially: Foster Aborn and Ginger Holbrook, Linda L. Bean, Robert and Nancy Briggs, Judith W. Canby, Ted and Terry Chaconas, John and Carolyn Coffee, Dr. Diane L. Colgan, Edmund and Leslie Cronin, Edith Dixon, Umberto Erculiani, Debbie Fleischaker, Stan Friedman and Janna Martin, Michael and Roberta Gardullo, Barbara Goodbody, Frank and Jean Heart, David H. Hickman, Treby and Arlene Johnson, Barry Kane and Karen Kessler, Christopher and Pamela Kloman, Agnes West Kohler, Cindy Lang, Kevin and Jan Lipson, Martha Lord, Andrew and Piezie Love, John and Vicky Manning, Judge Faye Martin, Susan and Steve Masone, Albert and Carla Massoni, Wilma Maust, David Palmer, Duer and Maryanne Pierce, Jonathan and Robin Plotkin, Christopher and Betsy Rector, Lois Rice, Richard and Madalyn Rockwell, Dr. Thomas J. and Ambassador Cynthia P. Schneider, Doc and Dean Schnurrenberger, Paul and Teena Shorb, George and Holly Stone, Robert and Heidi Stott, Gerald and Kristin Strid, Sadie Somerville and Rodney W. Jester, Richard and Karen Teller, Judith Tierno, Russ and Betty Tilly, Thomas and Cathy Tinsley, Donald and Laurel Weaver, Franz and Alice Weidemann, Richard and Elaine Whiting, and Steve and Lynn Zwecker.

Introduction

The counterpoint of the macrocosm and the microcosm, the vast and the minute, is a concept that has shaped the evolution of both art and science through the ages. It is very much at work today in the artistic visions of Greg Mort.

Some of Mort's paintings show a subtle interplay of the extremes, while in others a singular majestic scene dominates. In many works he focuses the viewer's attention on seemingly commonplace objects that, upon further study, reveal a much deeper meaning.

Works that transmit a sense of the immensity of the universe are exemplified by the painting *Stream of Stars;* the Milky Way, in all its dazzling brightness, seems to flow through a deep sea of blue with a shell-strewn beach in the foreground. In the symbology created by Greg Mort, the shells testify to the very presence of life, and the Milky Way is a link between Earth and sky. In his creation *Under a Billion Suns,* the vast depth of the celestial vault and the grand sweep of time are confronted by a single earthbound Tulip Shell.

Man's relationship with the universe has inspired Mort since his early work, as in the 1988 watercolor *Into the Night,* where a young man sitting on rocks contemplates a night sky full of stars. Although rendered with a very different pictorial style, Marc Chagall's 1910 *Figure in Front of the Blue Vault* creates the same sensation and can be considered an anticipation of Mort's sensibility.

The microcosm aspect of Mort's artistic world is illustrated by his rendition of a silver spoon that cradles miniature shells (*Silver Spoon*); by a collection of rocks and shells—and one miniature moon—carefully balanced in a latticework of sticks (*Sticks and Stones*); by a stamped envelope celebrating the Apollo moon landing (*Special Delivery*); and by an intriguing apple, suspended at the border of an embroidered tablecloth and challenging the laws of gravity (*Second Dream*).

Three scenes in which Mort paints the Moon at play with the clouds (*The Shining Sea, Ring Around the Moon,* and *Silver Ribbon*) recall a time four centuries ago when, in 1609, the German painter Adam Elsheimer produced one of the very first examples of the naturalistic nocturnal landscape. Accurately depicting the constellations in the sky, it would stand as a prototype for the great masters who came after him—Greg Mort among them. The title of Elsheimer's painting is *The Flight into Egypt,* and as with Mort's work, the Moon, the stars and the Milky Way dominate the scene.

Mort's voyages through powerful landscapes—where the earthly elements of water, stone and evergreen vibrate in unison with the imposing aspects of the night sky (*Forever Maine, Northern Comet, River of Night*)—bring us to a heightened sense of being part of the Cosmos.

As an astronomer, I am thankful that Greg Mort is inspired in part by the same events and heavenly bodies that I study. The collection of images in *Voyages* invites everyone to share in his passionate appreciation of the world around him—from swirling galaxies to spiraling shells, and from the glacier-carved coastline of Maine to the hand-sewn lacework of an heirloom tablecloth. Enjoy the journey.

Francesco Bertola
Professor of Astrophysics, The University of Padua
Author, *Via Lactea: The Milky Way in History and in the Heavens*

Night into Day

watercolor
21" x 28" . 2004
Collection of Debbie Fleischaker

Most of us exist in a daytime world. We think of the day as a kind of "reality." And yet the day is, in many ways, a deceit. What we really see during the daytime hours is an ocean of air illumined by the Sun and creating a wonderful canopy of blue—a comforting presence not unlike the blanket we wrapped up in as a child. Only at night do we see the true world before us: a vast, ancient, star-studded abyss. Some part of us resists the notion of a dark universe. Even this painting, *Night into Day,* betrays my subconscious belief in a sunlit Cosmos: In reality, the day should be folding back to reveal the night.

Stream of Stars

watercolor
28" x 28" . 1984
Collection of Mr. and Mrs. John D. Coffee

From our Earthly perspective at the edge of the galaxy, the Milky Way flows as a sparkling golden river across the night sky. That was the view from the dawn of time until 1609, when Galileo first trained a telescope on the heavens. *Stream of Stars* pays tribute to that grand sweep of time.

It also refers to the kinship between the oceans of Earth and the oceans of space, and how, just as our watery sea gave birth to life on Earth, the Milky Way gave birth to Earth itself. We, on our planet, are adrift in a sea of space in much the same way a seedpod floats in the oceans of Earth.

The painting's perspective—a snail's eye view from the beach, where the spiraling cases of shells mirror the churning spirals of the galaxies—brings the worlds of the finite and the infinite closer together.

SHADES OF NIGHT

watercolor
28" x 32" . 1998
Collection of Mr. and Mrs. Kevin Lipson

EAST OF MIDNIGHT

watercolor
21" x 28" . 1987
Collection of Linda L. Bean

Rhythm may seem more applicable to a composer than a painter, but art too must sing. In *Shades of Night* the visual rhythm lies in the repeated triangles of the fabric, the negative triangles between the shades, and the five negative triangles that outline each starfish. From this perspective, the composition is a symphony of triangles.

Forever Maine *oil*
30" x 40" . 2002
Collection of Mr. and Mrs. A. Duer Pierce III

The summer of 2002 marked my twenty-fifth year of painting in Maine, and I noted the anniversary with the large-scale oil on canvas *Forever Maine*. The glacier-scoured rocks and stately firs depicted here lead out to the Marshall Point Lighthouse, a few hundred yards from our summer home and studio in Port Clyde. With little ambient light by night, the locale gives full play to the starry sky. Fierce storms pound the rugged Maine coast relentlessly, but its granite bulwarks hold.

STEWARDSHIP II

watercolor
16" x 28" . 1996
Collection of Vice President and Mrs. Albert Gore.

After President Clinton acquired the original *Stewardship* watercolor in 1991 (page 56), it may have seemed unlikely that Vice President Al Gore also would come to own an original work. Then, in 1996 the National Democratic Committee asked me to create a special painting with an environmental theme that would be presented to the Vice President. I was familiar with Gore's book *Earth in the Balance*. In keeping with the concerns he expressed there, I chose to depict our fragile planet on shifting sands, an expression of the uncertainty that surrounds our environmental destiny.

The delicate glass sphere denotes the thin film that is our atmosphere, and the satin ribbon symbolizes the measurable damage we humans are inflicting on the world ecosystem—progressive effects revealed through scientific scrutiny and data.

The Vice President seemed genuinely surprised and pleased to receive the original watercolor, and I was thrilled to see *Stewardship II* in the hands of one so instrumental in alerting us to the perils Earth faces.

Vice President Al Gore and Mrs. Gore receiving Stewardship II from Greg.
Photograph courtesy of the Greg Mort Family Archives.

MUSSEL RIDGE
watercolor
21" x 28" . 1993
Collection of Mr. and Mrs. Christopher Kloman

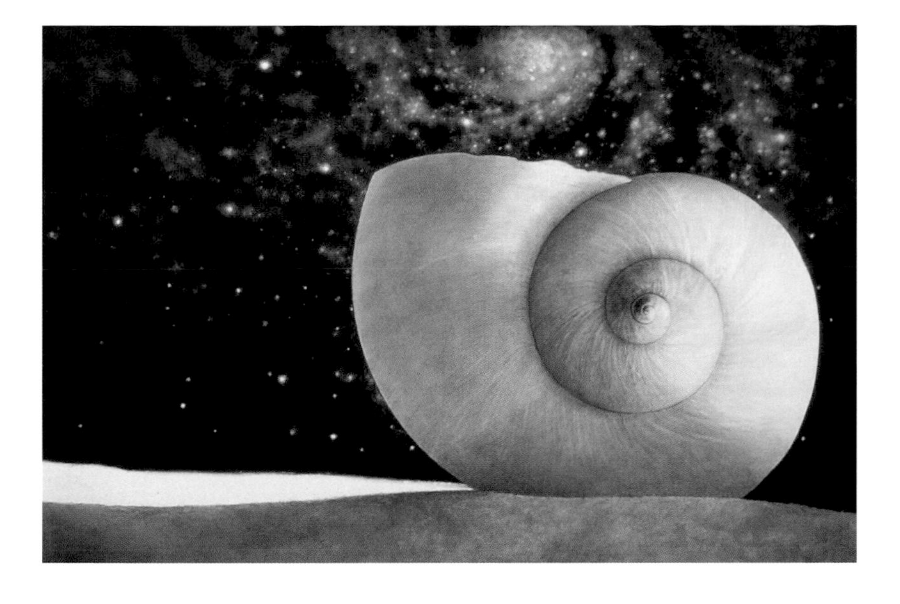

Spirals *watercolor*
21" x 28" . 1987
Collection of Barbara M. Goodbody

The spiral is one of the most ubiquitous patterns in nature. Found repeatedly in plants, animals and the heavens, it also enriches such sciences as biology, physics and mathematics. I see the spiral as one of the visual notes that compose the rhythm and harmony of the natural world.

As an artist, I try to use any pattern's manifestations as notes in a visual song, to create a tune that is at once fresh but familiar. After all, the same spiral that shapes a small shell and a vast galaxy also determines the arrangement of seeds on a pinecone and the swirl of water as it drains out of the kitchen sink. The great cosmic symphony is going on all around us.

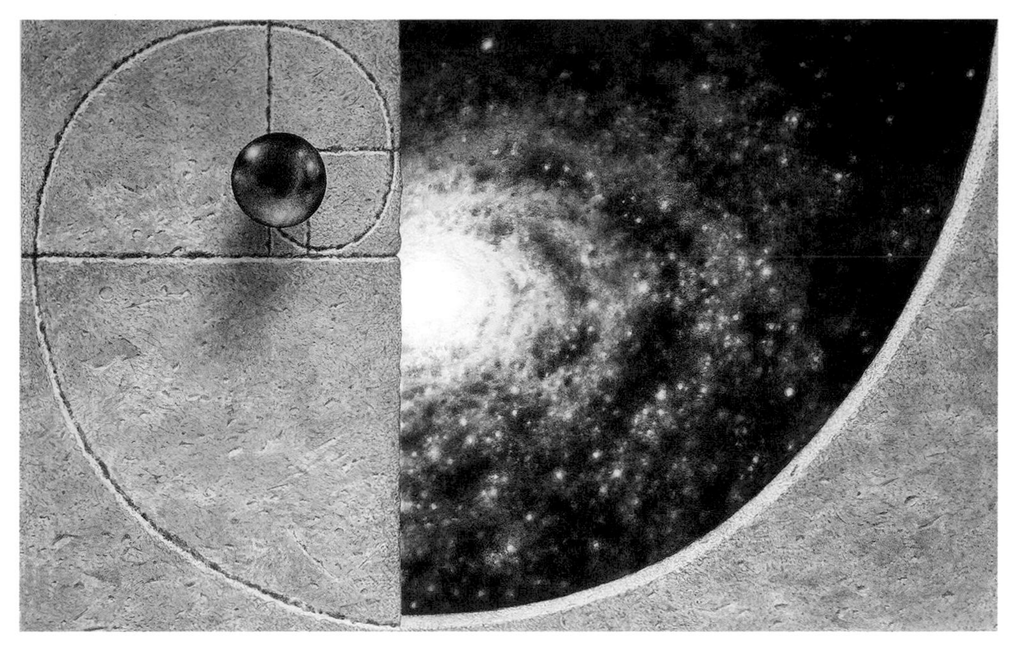

Golden Spiral *watercolor*
14" x 22" . 1999
Collection of David H. Hickman

This watercolor incorporates the Fibonacci ratio, also known as the golden ratio, into its proportions. The ratio is based on the Fibonacci sequence developed by brilliant twelfth-century mathematician Leonardo Fibonacci. It begins with the numbers 1, 1, 2. After that, each new figure is the sum of the previous two: 2+3=5, and 3+5=8, and so on (2,3,5,8,13,21,34, . . .). Further along, the Fibonacci ratio of 1:1.618 becomes apparent when any numeral is divided by its predecessor.

Drawing right-angle lines with one side 1.618 times longer than the other creates a perfect rectangle. And scribing a square within the rectangle—using the length of the shorter side—leaves another golden-ratio rectangle remaining. Repeating this pattern makes a series of ever-decreasing squares and golden-ratio rectangles. Arcs penned from the inward corner of the squares create the classic spiral. *Golden Spiral* celebrates this powerful mathematical expression, one of the fundamental underpinnings of nature.

EARTH FROM THE MOON

watercolor
21" x 28" . 1997
Collection of Mrs. Wilma Maust

COSMIC OCEAN

watercolor
21" x 28" . 1985
Private Collection

UNIVERSE UNFOLDING

watercolor
25" x 18" . 2002
Private Collection

DISTANT OCEANS

watercolor
28" x 21" . 1991
Collection of Scott Pitcock

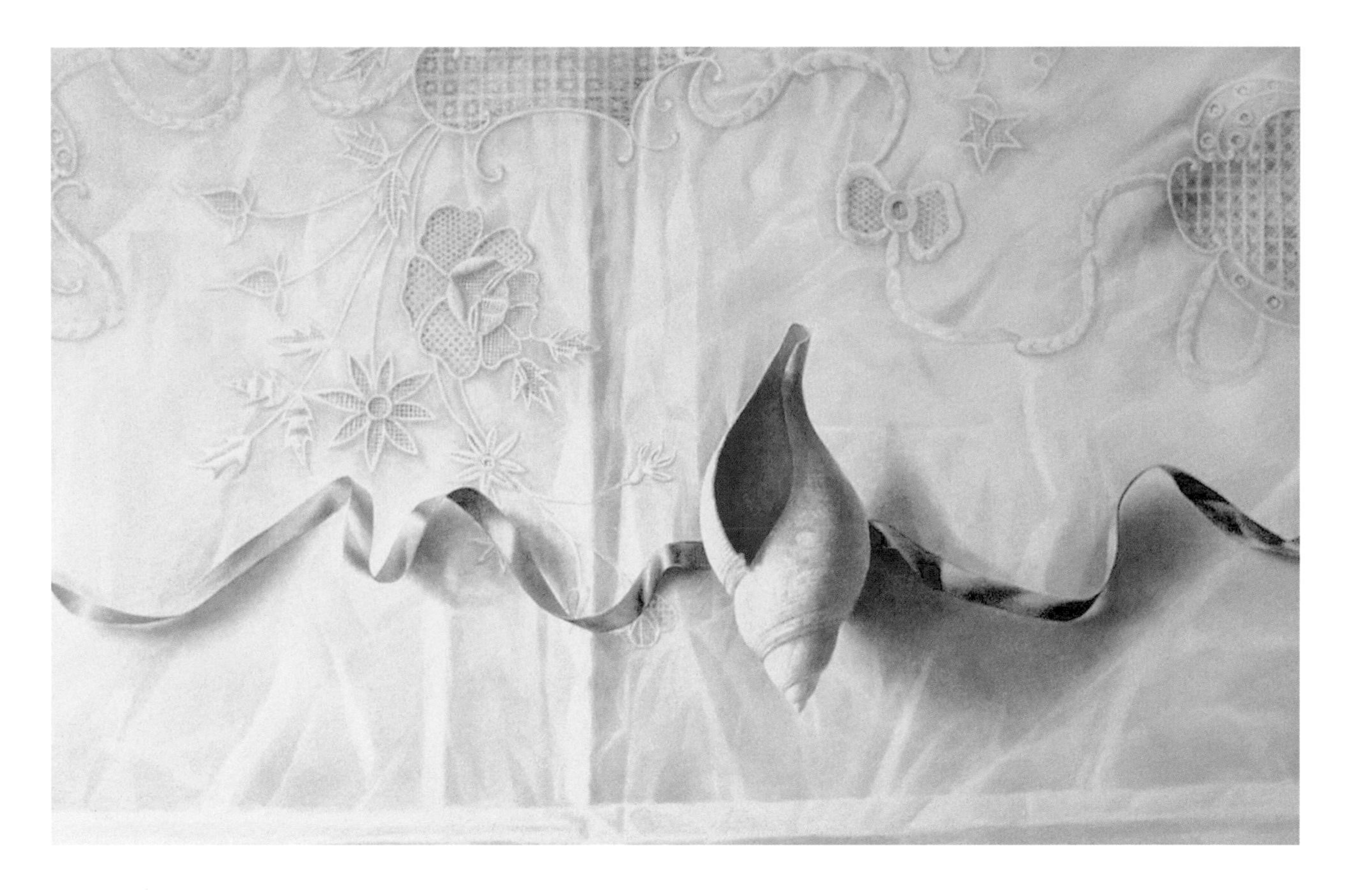

FINERY *watercolor*
21" x 28" . 1986
Collection of Mrs. Wilma Maust

STARRY POOL *watercolor*
21" x 28" . 1987
Collection of Mr. and Mrs. Richard P. Axten Family

CHANGE IN THE WEATHER *watercolor*
19" x 27" . 1989
Private Collection

EARTHSHINE-MOONSHINE
oil
14" x 18" . 2001
Collection of Linda Huber

Apollo 8

watercolor
33" x 26" . 1998
Collection of General and Mrs. William Anders

In December 1968, America's manned space program took a dramatic step. With the race to the Moon against the former Soviet Union ramping up, U.S. space officials decided to alter the existing schedule and push forward with a manned lunar orbital mission. *Apollo 8* still stands out as one of the most dramatic flights of the era—man's first venture beyond our home planet and into the gravitational grasp of another body. This milestone was made even more memorable by the enduring photo "Earth Rise," taken by crew member Colonel William Anders.

Thirty years later, it was my good fortune to meet Anders, now *General* Anders, through a mutual friend. He and his wife, Valerie, asked me to create a commemorative image of the mission. In that painting, the looping ribbon represents not only the number "8" but also the path to the moon and back. The crescent moon is shown as it appeared in the sky from Earth during the mission. Three starfish adorn the shores of Earth, one for each crewmember.

Fallen Star

watercolor
28" x 21" . 1995
Collection of Mr. and Mrs. Keith Stoltz

Our son Jonathan was 10 when I painted *Fallen Star*. We worked in the confines of my Maryland studio, but the setting portrayed is the Maine seacoast—never far from my mind. While Jonathan had been a model for several paintings, this one I considered a portrait; he, like his father, has a passion for scouring the beaches for "sea treasures." I like to think there's a curious child in all of us, delighting in discovery on a beach or along a roadside, hoping to capture a fallen star.

AURORA | *watercolor*
21" x 28" . 1990
Collection of Mr. and Mrs. Murray H. Witcher

Year of the Comet

watercolor
48" x 60" . 1985
Collection of the Smithsonian National Air and Space Museum

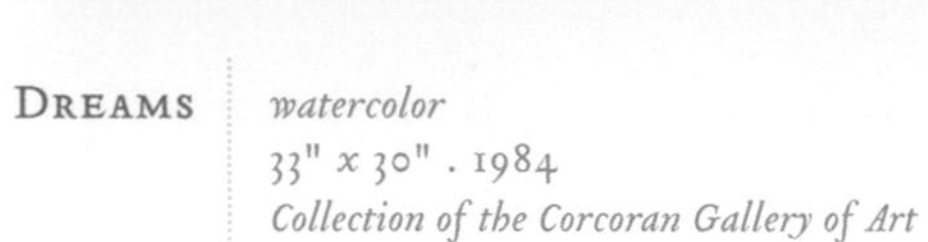

Dreams *watercolor*
33" x 30" . 1984
Collection of the Corcoran Gallery of Art

The concept for the watercolor *Dreams* began in a curious way. I had for several days noticed on the front seat of our family car a green plastic bag with something inside. A magazine, perhaps? The bag had a transparent quality, and through it I could make out a very interesting shape. Each time I returned to drive the car I took note of the flowing contours of the image, which in my mind were becoming a folded napkin.

Finally my curiosity got the better of me and I looked inside the bag. To my surprise, the curving shape I had seen was the back of a woman's dress, the upside-down V-shape of her back and shoulder blades outlined by red fabric. The green transparent plastic had cancelled out the redness of her dress, allowing only the shape of her back to show through. This realization did not dampen my enthusiasm for that wonderful triangle. It was like something out of a dream—there and yet not—and I was compelled to paint it.

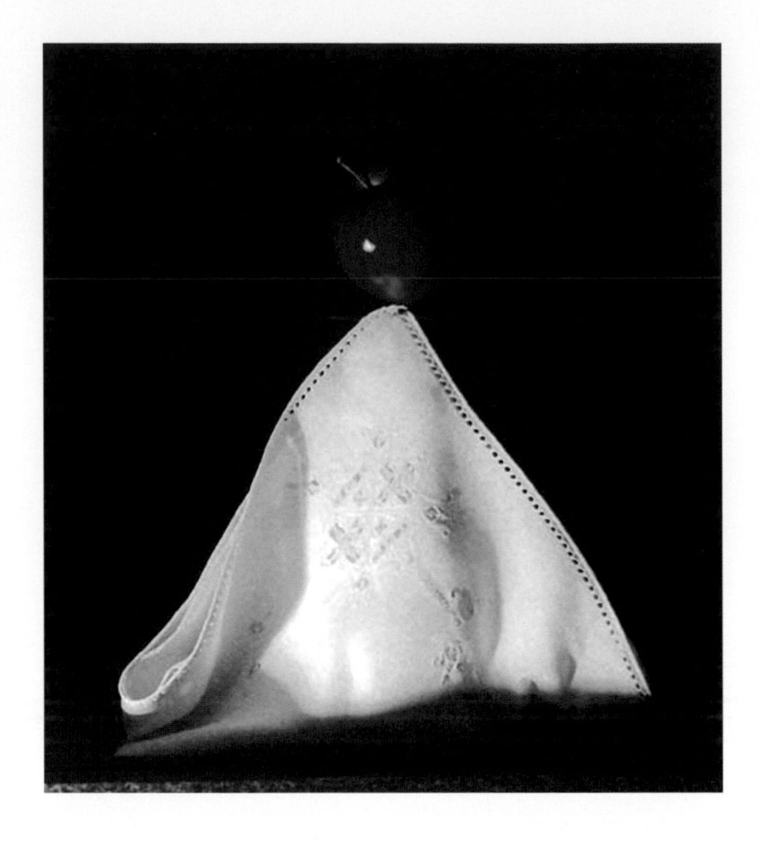

Second Dream *watercolor*
32" x 29" . 2005
Collection of David H. Hickman

More than twenty years after I painted *Dreams*, I returned to the concept with *The Second Dream*. This time, I took a more surreal approach. By moving the apple from its stable position on the table to the teetering heights of the folded napkin, I introduced anticipation and potential energy into the composition.

APPLE RINGS

watercolor
20" x 24" . 1999
Collection of Mr. Matthew Trone

By placing Saturn-like rings about an Earthly apple, I hoped to shrink the vast distance between these two planets. I also wanted to create a jarring collision of elements out of their normal context, which gives the painting a surrealistic quality. Before painting *Apple Rings*, I arranged the elements in my studio, fashioning Saturn's rings from paper cutouts. Doubtless the choice of an apple as the subject originated in my admiration for Isaac Newton and the falling fruit that inspired his notions about gravity. Otherwise, I suppose, I could just as easily have created a painting titled "Onion Rings."

NINE PLANETS *watercolor*
12" x 13" . 1993
Private Collection

DRAGON FLY *watercolor*
20" x 23" . 1993
Private Collection

If you visited my studio, you would find that most of the objects seen in my *trompe l'oeil* painting *Nine Planets* are part of my personal landscape. My avocation as an amateur astronomer has always blended with my vocation as a painter. This still-life puzzle invites the viewer in through a treasure hunt of easily recognizable images and symbols for the nine planets.

Mercury's symbol appears on the antique book latch. Venus is a word on the handle of the screwdriver. Earth is seen on the stamp below a space-walking Gemini astronaut. Mars is the image on the post card. Jupiter is hidden as the striped globe on the gourd, and Saturn is discernible on the color negative.

The symbol for Uranus is hidden on the backside of the playing card. Neptune's trident is carved into the brass key. Pluto (which the International Astronomical Union later demoted to "dwarf planet" status) is honored on the round key tag, which bears the initials of Percival Lowell, the planetary astronomer who initiated the search for its discovery.

GREEN LEAVES *watercolor*
17" x 23" . 2000
Private Collection

SATURN'S APPLE

watercolor
18" x 15" . 1999
Private Collection

STEWARDSHIP III

watercolor
21" x 28" . 2004
Private Collection

To go beyond *Stewardship* and *Stewardship II* (pages 56 and 13), I decided to expand the visual story line of the Earth as an apple by creating the painterly equivalent of a prequel. *Stewardship III* shows the birth of the metaphor, with the apple skin being peeled away to unveil, or birth, the Earth.

STAR STRUCK *watercolor*
21" x 28" . 1999
Collection of Kathleen Kolpik

FRAGILE EARTH *watercolor*
21" x 21" . 2003
Collection of Scott and Cynthia Smith

The Morning Sun *watercolor*
21" x 28" . 1985
Private Collection

Across the Sea *oil*
25" x 52" . 2006
Collection of Mr. and Mrs. Michael Liman

Temptation *watercolor*
21" x 28" . 1982
Collection of David and Jane Appenbrink

The waters that break onto the Maine Coast are numbingly cold, even on warm summer days. Still, as midday temperatures climb into the 80's, the temptation to take a dip in the inviting saltwater inlets is strong. By the time the ankles are submerged, reason takes hold. This painting captures that moment between temptation and restraint.

My wife, Nadine, posed for long minutes as I created a life drawing with pencil and paper for *Temptation*. It was a race against the incoming tide and Nadine's inevitable fatigue from holding her arms in position. Over the years, an ability to remember information such as color and small detail has allowed me to complete a painting without returning to the spot where the inspiration was first born. Likewise, I never tamper with any study done on location; it has a quality that is unique to that moment in time alone.

SOLITAIRE *watercolor*
28" x 21" . 2004
Private Collection

Solitaire

A ragged little tree grows on Brothers Island
Its sturdy trunk bent against the wind.
Half of it is dead,
Cloaked in gray-green lichen.
The other half thrives;
Green, glossy needles
Winking at the crescent moon.
This tree springs from
Hardy Juniper, blueberry and gorse
Which cling in profusion
To the granite bed.
I am that tree,
Grown bent without breaking,
My feet of granite bathed by the sea
And moonbeams crowning my hair.

– Jean Diemert

There's a weather-worn spruce near our summer home that's become something of an icon in my work. It's on one of a pair of tiny Maine islands known to locals as "The Brothers," separated at high tide and joined at low. My family and I have traveled there countless times to paint, picnic and absorb the natural beauty. There are no manmade objects on The Brothers; only a record of ancient glacial movements etched in granite, and plant life determined to survive in the harsh winter environment.

Even from the mainland, you can see the outline of this lonely tree, sculpted by the wind and silhouetted against the sky. Over the twenty-five summers I have drawn and painted that tree in works such as *Solitaire*, it has come to represent for me the persistence of life and the fierce adaptability of nature.

STARS AT SEA *oil*
24" x 24" . 2006
Collection of Steven and Lynn Zwecker

PAPER TIGER

watercolor
12" x 19" . 1984
Collection of Cindy Lang

I sometimes feel the need to challenge myself and approach a subject from a new angle that surprises both me and the viewer. In the case of *Paper Tiger*, I first painted a Tiger Swallowtail butterfly in watercolor, then carefully cut it out and placed it on a fine linen cloth. When I executed the still life, I was in essence painting my painting of the insect; so the title made perfect sense.

THE BEACON

watercolor
18" x 24" . 1986
Collection of Ted and Terry Chaconas

Specimens *watercolor*
21" x 28" . 1989
Collection of Robert and Amy Campbell

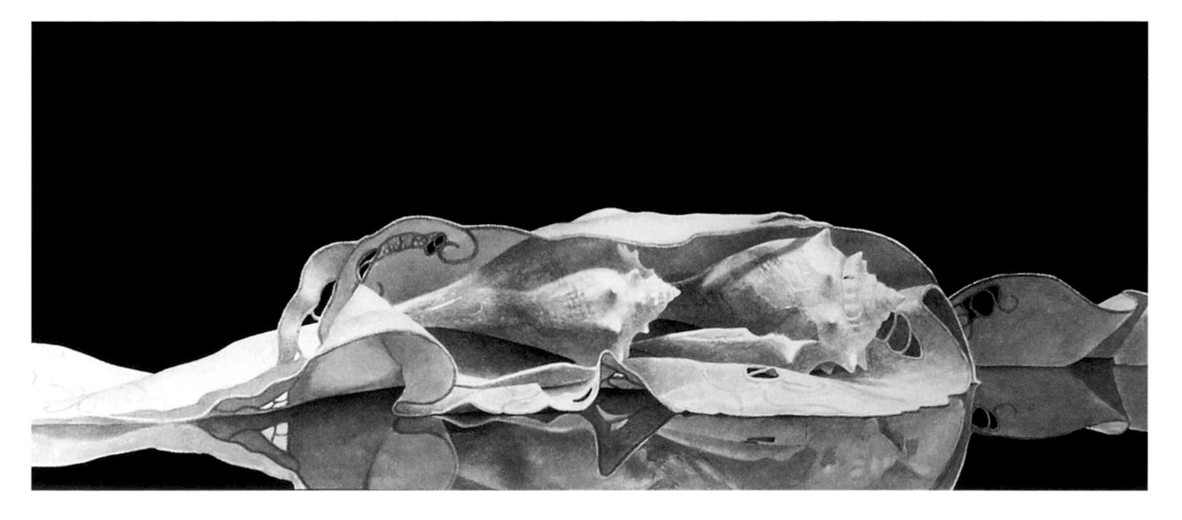

Wave *watercolor*
21" x 28" . 1992
Private Collection

Above the Deep *watercolor*
26" x 33" . 1993
Collection of Mr. and Mrs. Kevin Lipson

LOWLAND SEA | *watercolor*
21" x 28" . 2002
Collection of Tom and Catherine Tinsley

IVY LACE | *watercolor*
21" x 22" . 1984
Collection of Jacqueline Cecil

VOYAGERS *watercolor*
32" x 40" . 1983
Collection of Linda L. Bean

Voyagers

Early in NASA's manned space program, the folks in charge had the wisdom to insist that events be recorded not only mechanically via camera and film, but also artistically through pencils, paint and sculpture. In 1983 I had the good fortune to be one of seven artists commissioned to record the historic launch of astronaut Sally Ride aboard the space shuttle *Challenger*. Our group of artists had amazing access to areas at the Kennedy Space Center rarely seen by the public, including the "white rooms" where spacecraft are assembled in incredibly clean environments.

The sketching and watercolor studies I brought home from those three wondrous, mind-boggling days inspired no less than ten polished paintings. These works are now displayed in NASA's fine art collection at Cape Canaveral and in the Smithsonian Institution's National Air and Space Museum in Washington, D.C.

Later that same year, when I began working on a series of Down East dory images, my mind would wander back to those precious hours at Cape Canaveral. The twin boats of my painting *Voyagers* became icons of the identical *Voyager 1* and *Voyager 2* spacecraft launched from Earth to explore the outer planets in 1976. The scene also came to represent all voyagers, past and present; the whiteness and purity of those rooms at the Cape; and the purity of the impulse that drives our species to explore.

Voyagers

Greg Mort's white boats
on white float through
my head this absolutely
still morning in which
a sheen of yellow pollen
lies across the lake. I
have a chill from a swim.
A sweatshirt will do, a
slice too of bread, Carolyn's
Maine berries jam, a cup of
black Malabar from Ellsworth.
Why do these boats stay
with me? Solitary shapes,
two punts propped in
one print upright against
a white clapboard barn
rendered lineless: one boat
down in another, waterless,
awash in a white sea, an
absence of human shapes,
lines so fine, themselves
the boat, the purveyors
of silence, a slight eroti-
cism in the shape and
silences. Where did we
see them first? That thin
rambling white clapboard
gallery in Port Clyde? It
was autumn. The care-
taker closing for the year.
"He's a lovely man," she
said. "You could write him."
I didn't but wish I did. Ellen
said he has stars in his head,
the very ones that wash down
a blue-black sky to a planet
of shells, celestial compost,
everywhere the shellfish
sea, though not (maybe so)
selfish, a sea without watery
blues: whites' silvers all in a
sea without salt in the print
she bought without haggling.
Imagine that: timorous. I
prefer to bargain. The danger
here is emptiness, the expec-
tation of risk is exciting though;
and the trick is to be as serene
as a white page, or a dirt road
cut through a stand of white
pines gone silver in a slow
morning mist: illusory haze.
What a trick to get carried
away in those little dreams
into which I'd love to be placed
as I'd love to be painted white
into the single boat, the lines
of oars in the shape of my hands
on a sea of handmade paper, white
of course, at least for today, Greg
Mort Day.

—Anthony Petrosky

Mirrored Islands

watercolor
26" x 33" . 1989
Collection of Frank Cantor and Esmeralda Santiago

Anyone who has spent time on the coast of Maine will appreciate the sense of drama and mystery that rolls in with the fog. The grey-white vapors can feel thick as soup for days at a time, then burn off in a matter of minutes to reveal a sparkling sunny day. Combined with the extreme tidal forces, this dramatic variation in the land- and seascape makes the Down East region an artist's paradise.

The day I painted *Mirrored Islands,* the islands looked like they were floating in the sky, and an eerie imaginary line seemed to delineate where the water stopped and the air began.

ANCHOR STONE *watercolor*
21" x 28" . 2002
Collection of Mr. and Mrs. Frank Heart

Last Wave *watercolor*
21" x 28" . 1981
Collection of Gregory and Laurie Hunt

It was a cold April when my wife, Nadine, and I arrived on Fishers Island off the coast of Connecticut. I had been invited by a collector of my work who owned a lovely home there to travel to the island and paint what interested me. Because it was off-season, there was almost no one else on the island. As I spent the first day or two getting my bearings, I was struck not only by the high number of gulls but also by how tame they were. They were infinitely more relaxed than those I had known in Maine.

Seeing this as a rare opportunity, I made many a study of the gulls in pencil and watercolor. The week flew by. In the end, the piece I believed to be the most successful was *The Last Wave*, a portrait of one large bird that seemed as fascinated with me as I was with it.

Upon returning to Maryland, I contacted the gentleman who had initiated the trip, excited to show him what I had produced. As he viewed the work, a terrified look came over his face and he became physically sick. How could I have known that as a child he had been viciously attacked by gulls on that very island?

Against the Tide *watercolor*
21" x 28" . 2000
Collection of Mr. Paul C. Dalrymple

RIVER OF LIFE *watercolor*
26" x 33" . 1988
Collection of Frank Cantor and Esmeralda Santiago

Sands of Time | *watercolor*
28" x 22" . 1999
Private Collection

On *The River of Life*

Walking along the rocky coast of Maine, I pine for that other sea, the Caribbean that rolls upon the shores of the island that nurtured me. I long for the colors of the tropics, the turquoise water, purple dawns over green mountains veiled with mist, frothy white foam along pink sands. Far beyond the horizon, Port Clyde's cold, gray sea becomes the warm, blue waters around Puerto Rico, a sparkling ocean teeming with multicolored life. But on this shore, a handful of shells, nestled within the pale folds of a whitework embroidery napkin, bring me back home, like an embrace.

—Esmeralda Santiago

Whorls *watercolor*
21" x 28" . 1989
Private Collection

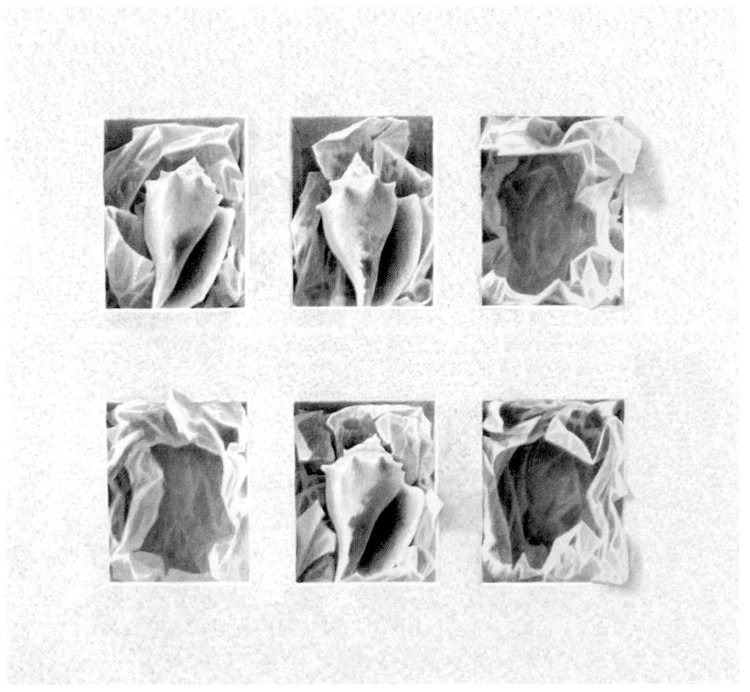

Time Passages *watercolor*
19" x 19" . 1993
Private Collection

LIGHTSCAPES *watercolor*
18" x 24" . 1989
Private Collection

CAPELLA *watercolor*
21" x 28" . 2004
Collection of Debbie Fleischaker

STEWARDSHIP

watercolor
14" x 18" . 1991
Collection of President and Mrs. William Clinton

The apple is an object I return to repeatedly in my work for both literal representation and as a metaphor. With each use, it has grown as an artistic signature and deepened in symbolic significance. The painting *Stewardship* began as an exercise in stretching my limits with this common motif. The idea was sparked in part by the lyrics of Michael Legrand's song "Windmills of Your Mind," which includes the phrase, "And the world is like an apple twirling silently in space."

When *Stewardship* was completed, with Earth painted on a highly perishable apple, viewers reacted quickly. What followed was one of those magical moments in art when a work takes on a life of its own. Many instantly interpreted the piece as a statement about the fragility of Earth, our environmental struggles and our inadequate stewardship of the home planet. The blank price tag, which I had added mainly as an element of texture, assumed greater symbolic value as well.

This image is a personal statement born of the Space Age, when we first saw our planet from afar and realized our tenuous place in the universe. We face major questions of sustainability and realize our survival depends on answers not yet found. The price of self-preservation? Nobody can be sure. What does seem clear, though, is that this world is more frail and delicate than we once thought. Like a piece of fruit, it is beautiful but easily bruised.

Stewardship was hanging in the home of Tom and Cynthia Schneider when President Bill Clinton first saw it in 1992. When his interest in the painting became apparent, the generous hosts decided to make it a gift to the First Family. The painting was taken from the wall and placed in the presidential limousine.

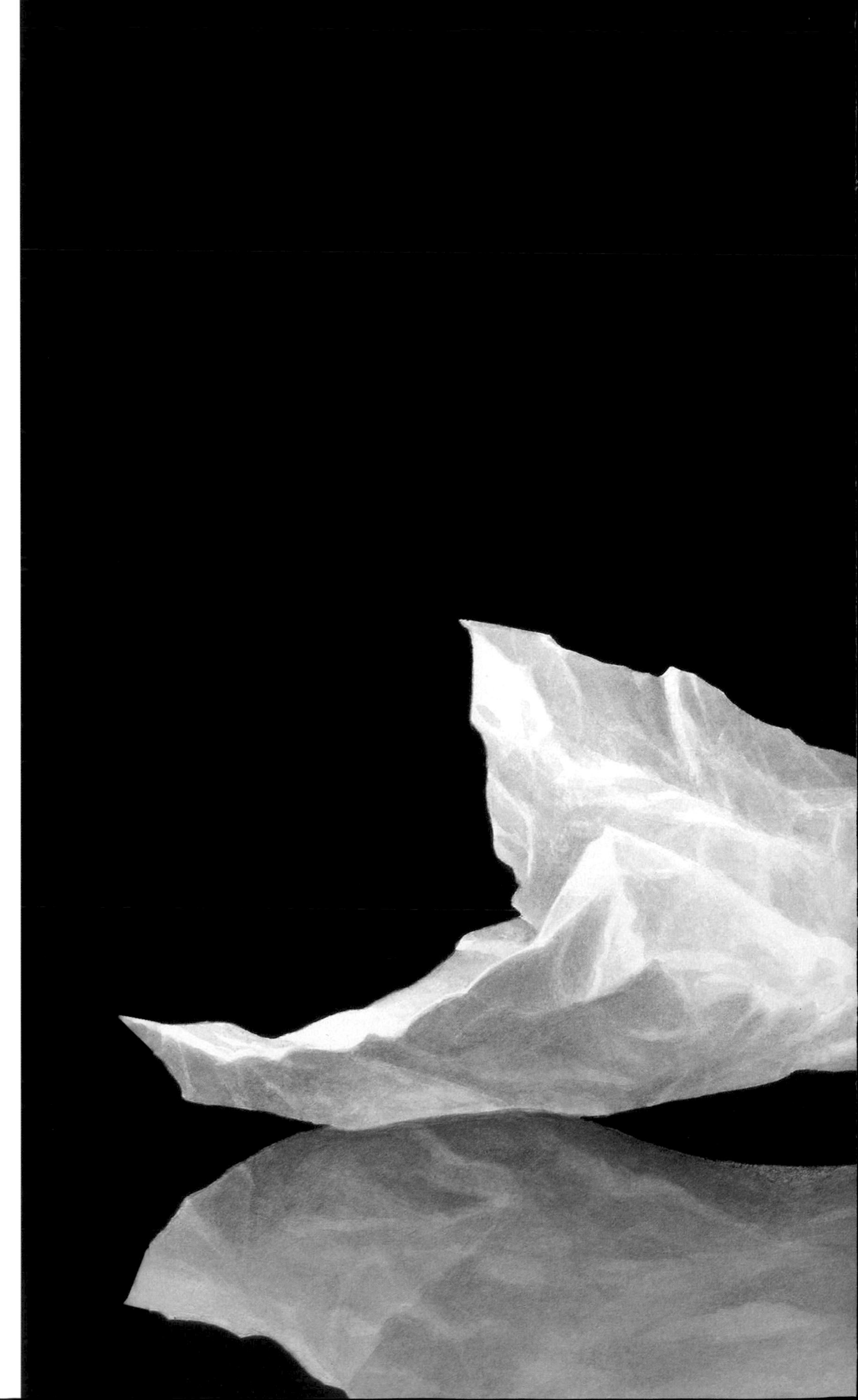

ISLAND GOODBYE | *watercolor*
30" x 40" . 1982
Private Collection

Island Goodbye

By the time I had a second opportunity to visit mid-coast Maine, in 1978, I had made a small number of friends there. Among them were the Whiteheads, who then owned Southern Island, near Tenants Harbor in Penobscot Bay. The lighthouse on the seaward edge of the small isle hadn't been in operation for many years, but it still stood proud and in good condition.

I could row a small boat out to Southern Island in less than 15 minutes. Once there, I found near-perfect privacy and a treasure trove for a young artist. After pulling the skiff ashore, I would make the inclined walk up to a meadow scattered with random spruce. Continuing to the top of the hill, I'd see the light itself, visible like the distant mast of a schooner at sea. By the time the keeper's house was in full view, the panorama was complete.

On sun-drenched mornings, the illumination defined the geometry of the buildings and painted the ocean an azure blue with a satiny horizon. For three summers, I would return many times to this paradise to work, each visit more fantastic than the last. Finally, and sadly for me, the island changed owners and my adventures there came to an end. Still, I longed to paint one last tribute to the place that had inspired me in infinite ways. By building a scale model of one corner of it—with house, light, meadow and rocky shore—I was able to fly above it like a lone gull heading out to sea. From that vantage point I was able to express my *Island Goodbye.*

Stone's Throw *oil*
24" x 32" . 2006
Collection of Mr. and Mrs. Pierce K. Crompton

Over Flow *watercolor*
21" x 28" . 1994
Collection of Lois D. Rice

SATURN'S GATE *watercolor*
18" x 26" . 1996
Collection of Diane L. Colgan M.D.

THE GREAT RIFT *watercolor*
25" x 19" . 1989
Private Collection

Murex | *watercolor*
18" x 28" . 1992
Collection of Harms-Townsend

The Sun, the Moon and the Stars

I never understood him

Every evening
He would abandon life
On this Earth
Turn his mind
To the vain
Celestial diamonds
That are the stars

Sipping espresso
Flavored with sugar
And moonlight
He would trace the paths
Of the constellations
Until the sun
Stole them from the sky

His routine
Was older than the
Sun-faded volumes
That took on the life
Of scripture
To him

Astronomy became
His religion

I had my suspicions
That he did not seek
To find himself
In his pursuit
Of Orion
Hercules
And Lyra

Rather that
He sought asylum
From his own faithless dreams

– Heather Doyle

Heather Doyle was 16 when a school assignment required her to write a poem inspired by a painting. She chose ***The Sun, the Moon and the Stars***, which she saw hanging in the Carla Massoni Gallery in Chestertown, Maryland. Her English teacher kindly forwarded the beautiful poem to me. – G.M.

The Sun, the Moon and the Stars

watercolor
21" x 25" . 1999
Collection of Stan and Kathleen Fox

SUMMER TIDE *watercolor*
21" x 28" . 1983
Collection of Cindy Lang

PENTAGRAM *watercolor*
21" x 28" . 1987
Private Collection

LAND'S END LIGHT

watercolor
21" x 28" . 1989
Private Collection

One of the most rewarding moments in the creative process comes when you are able to go beyond the everyday point of view. Such an opportunity arose with the wonderful Marshall Point Light, which is located just a few hundred yards from my summer studio in Port Clyde, Maine. The landmark has undoubtedly been drawn, photographed, and painted tens of thousands of times. I took it as a personal challenge to portray it in a less-than-obvious way. On a still July morning, when my children and I set out to explore the tide pools below the light, this new perspective presented itself.

LEEWARD *watercolor*
26" x 37" . 2005
Collection of Michael and Roberta Gardullo

In 1988, after a decade of returning to Maine each summer to paint, we settled at the very end of the St. George peninsula in the fishing village of Port Clyde. Local craftsmen helped us restore Fieldstone Castle and make it our home.

Each morning at dawn, I walked along the shore with my three dogs and watched the local fishermen stream out of the harbor. One lobster boat stood out among all others. It was a smaller, older craft with an unusual triangle of sail near the stern and it fished just off the road to the Marshall Point Light.

As the years passed I came to know its captain, Fred Lord, and his wife, Mary. I learned that the lovely little sail, called a "jigger," is an old-timer's trick that stabilizes the boat and helps it stay turned into the wind.

One day, I saw Fred's little boat positioned against a band of fog on the leeward of two islands known as "The Brothers." The resulting watercolor, *Leeward*, is my tribute not just to Fred and Mary Lord, but to all the lobstermen (and women) who make their living from the sea.

STAR BIRTH | *watercolor*
21" x 28" . 2003
Private Collection

One summer afternoon in Maine, my eyes fell upon an almost pure white stone on the shoreline. Picking it up, I noticed that the bright sunlight shone through it, creating a sublime glow. It was as if my quartz treasure were alive.

I thought about the first life on Earth and wondered, was it like the phosphorescence visible in the ocean at night? I began to ponder the creation of the planets and stars, themselves.

Back in my studio, I constructed the still life for *Star Birth.* I buried a small bright light in a bed of sand, and then placed the piece of quartz on top. The effect was amazing. It was July of 2003, and as I painted I remembered that in August the planet Mars would pass closer to Earth than it had in more than 50,000 years. As a tribute to that astronomical event, I included a small replica of the red planet in the foreground at lower left.

Amber Sky *oil*
21" x 40" . 2003
Private Collection

COLLECTED LIGHT

watercolor
20" x 26" . 2004
Collection of Judith E. Tierno

It was the day of the celestial Equinox, spring of 2004, and the north-climbing sun flooded with new warmth into my Maryland studio. Like a stage spotlight, it focused on a white shell in my collection, creating a study of light and dark. I added the butterfly to contrast hard and soft, as well. That butterfly, and the prospect of lengthening days, stirred my anticipation of summer, when my family and I would be winging our way to Maine.

Island Guardian | *oil*
30" x 40" . 2005
Collection of Umberto Erculiani

When the great ice sheets departed North America some ten thousand years ago, they left a huge boulder perched on a rocky ledge of Mosquito Island, just off the coast of Port Clyde, Maine. Geologists call dislocated pieces of rock like this one "glacial erratics," because they have been brought from afar and are so different from the other rocks in their surroundings.

As big as a house, the Mosquito Island erratic is easy to spy from the water; in fact, it's even visible in satellite images taken from space. The boulder's surface is speckled in a weatherworn assemblage of lichen and erosion, a testimony to the millions of days and nights it has lain in the elements. During that vast sweep of time, the familiar constellations have wandered into the positions we see today.

To recognize that grand passage of time and that endurance, I incorporated astronomical mementos into the historical record already etched into the rock's textured skin.

CONSTELLATION *oil*
18" x 24" . 2006
Collection of Michael and Lorrie Landsberg

My love affair with astronomy has led me to incorporate celestial references into my paintings that are not at once obvious to the viewer. The oil painting *Constellation* is a good example: Tiny planets and stars are hidden among the shell fragments and sand. The contrived arrangement of the starfish is an allusion to man's desire to impose order on the universe through devices such as mapping and labeling the constellations.

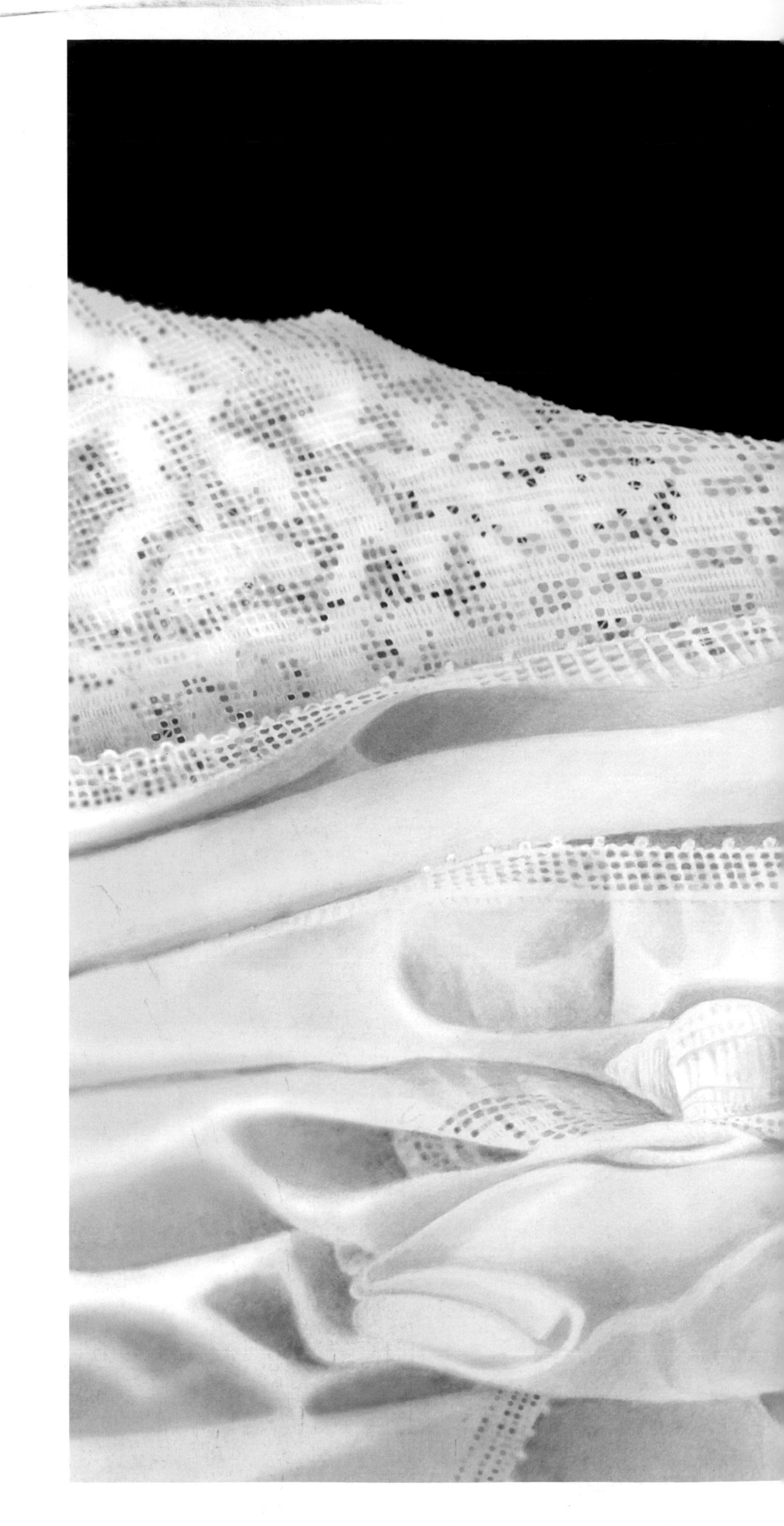

COLLECTION IN WHITE
watercolor
21" x 28" . 1993
Private Collection

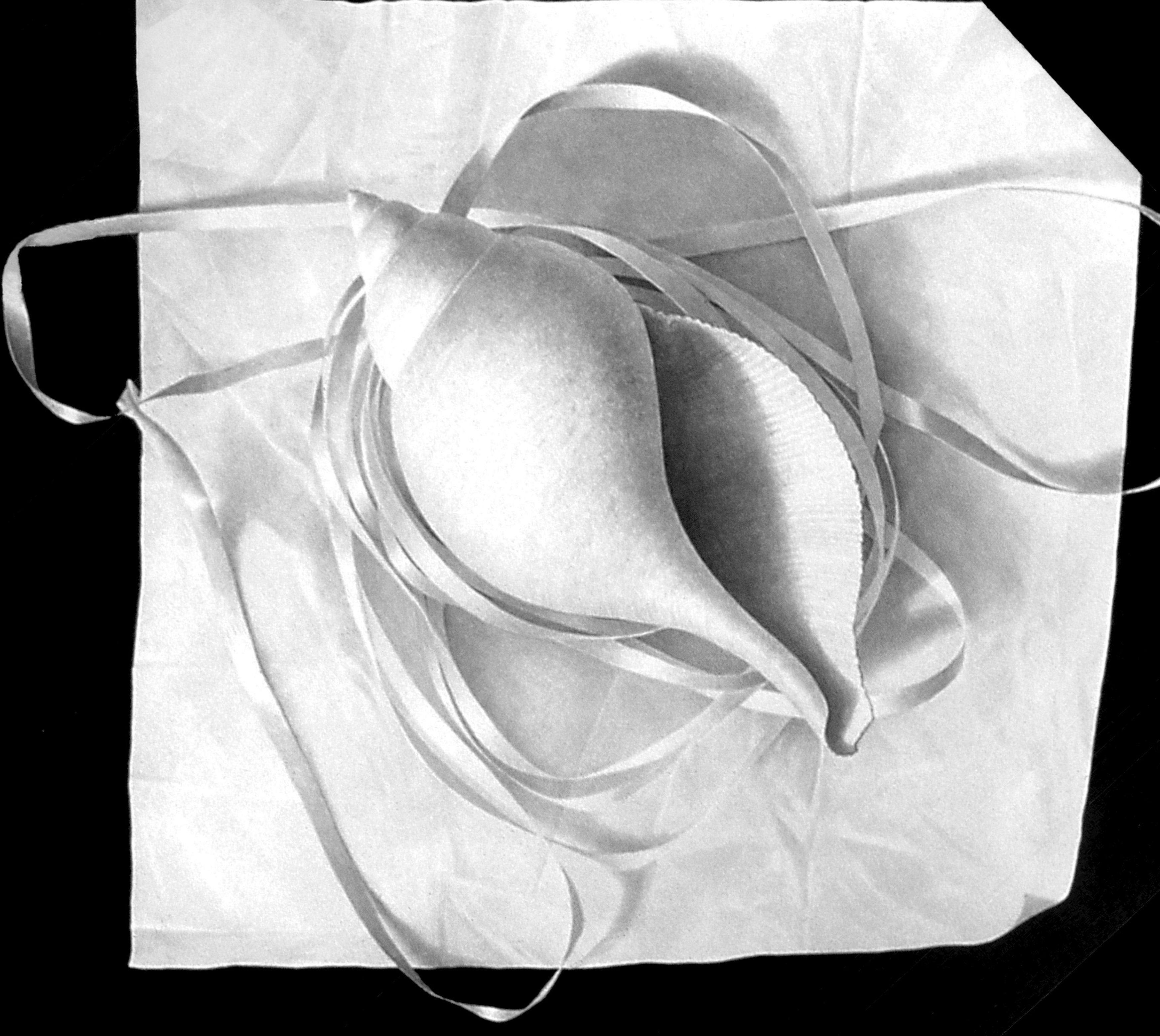

MORNING SUN | *watercolor*
20" x 25" . 1999
Private Collection

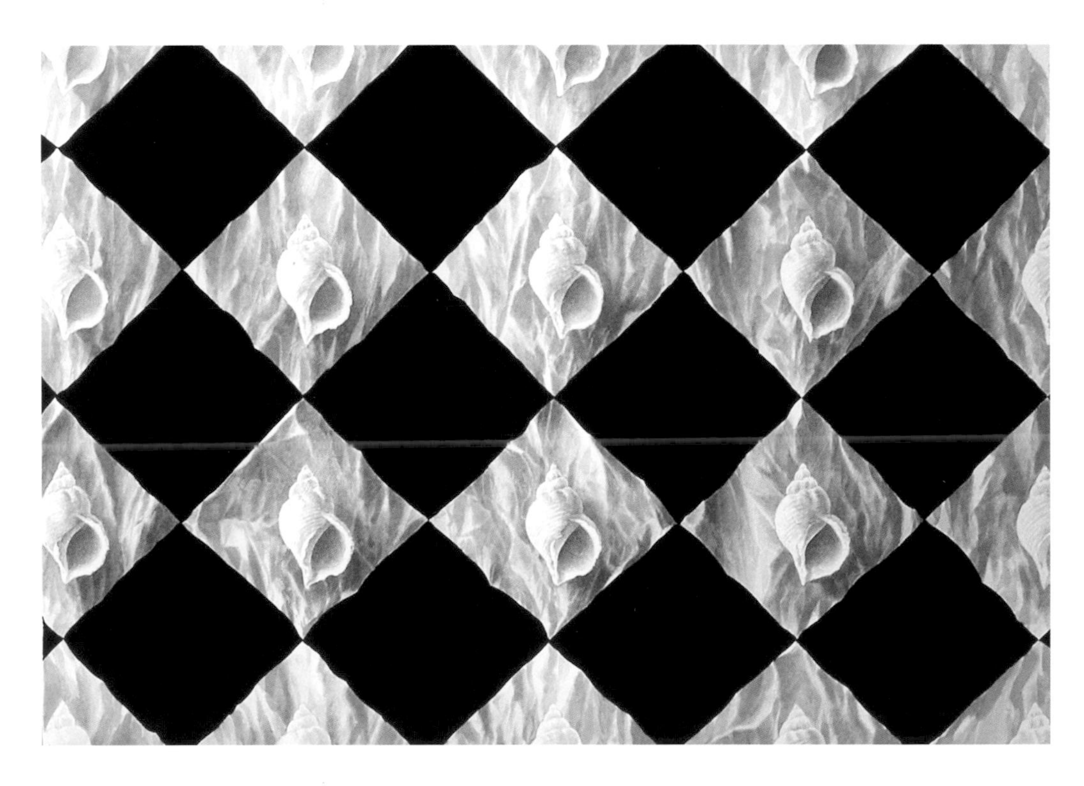

WORLDS WITHOUT END | *watercolor*
21" x 28" . 1996
Private Collection

INFINITY | *watercolor*
33" x 26" . 1987
Private Collection

SILVER AND GOLD *watercolor*
21" x 25" . 1999
Collection of Peter and Kathy Hickling

VENETIAN *watercolor*
21" x 25" . 1997
Private Collection

NIGHT TIDE *watercolor*
26" x 34" . 1986
Private Collection

PATTERNS *watercolor*
28" x 21" . 1992
Collection of Jonathan and Robin Plotkin

Night Visitor

watercolor
26" x 32" . 1999
Private Collection

For sky watchers around the world, 1996 was the Year of the Comets. Excitement ran high as astronomers cheered the end of a twenty-year drought of major comets. First came Hyakutake, sweeping near the Earth and sporting a gossamer tail that looked fifty times larger than the apparent width of the moon. Soon after, Hale-Bopp graced first the morning, then the evening skies, for many weeks.

The call of the comets to an artist and astronomer was loud and irresistible. It fueled my fascination with the universe and humankind's position in it. *Night Visitor* juxtaposes a luminous visitor from outer space with a metaphorical seashell caged within a glass shell.

The glass ball is meant to echo the dazzling coma surrounding comets, but it also speaks to their soap-bubble fragility—a property not always understood. In 1910, when scientists suggested the Earth would pass through the tail of Comet Halley, the prospect stirred panicked purchases of gas masks and anti-comet pills. Now we know that a comet tail millions of miles long contains a lower density of matter than does the purest vacuum produced by man.

MOON AND STAR
watercolor
22" x 28" . 1987
Collection of Mr. and Mrs. Alvin Curkin

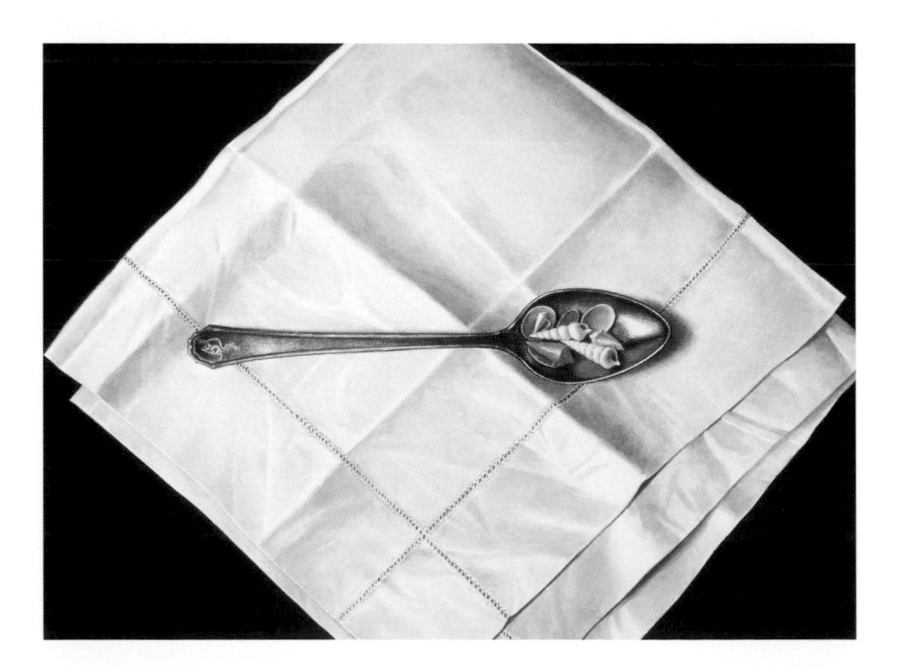

SILVER SPOON
watercolor
21" x 28" . 2000
Collection of Mr. and Mrs. Joseph DiNunno

RIVER OF NIGHT

watercolor
28" x 21" . 1994
Collection of Nathan J. Clark

Earth's spectacular, ancient view of the Milky Way has been honored and represented by artists throughout time. For many cultures around the globe, it has been a symbol for creation itself. As cities and suburban areas grow, the amount of ambient light increases and we lose more of our starry sky heritage. The sad result: Several generations have grown up having never seen the full glory of their own galactic home.

Fortunately, there's growing awareness of so-called light pollution. Through education and better designs in illumination, we can take back the night and ensure that future generations will be able to experience first-hand the mighty *River of Night*.

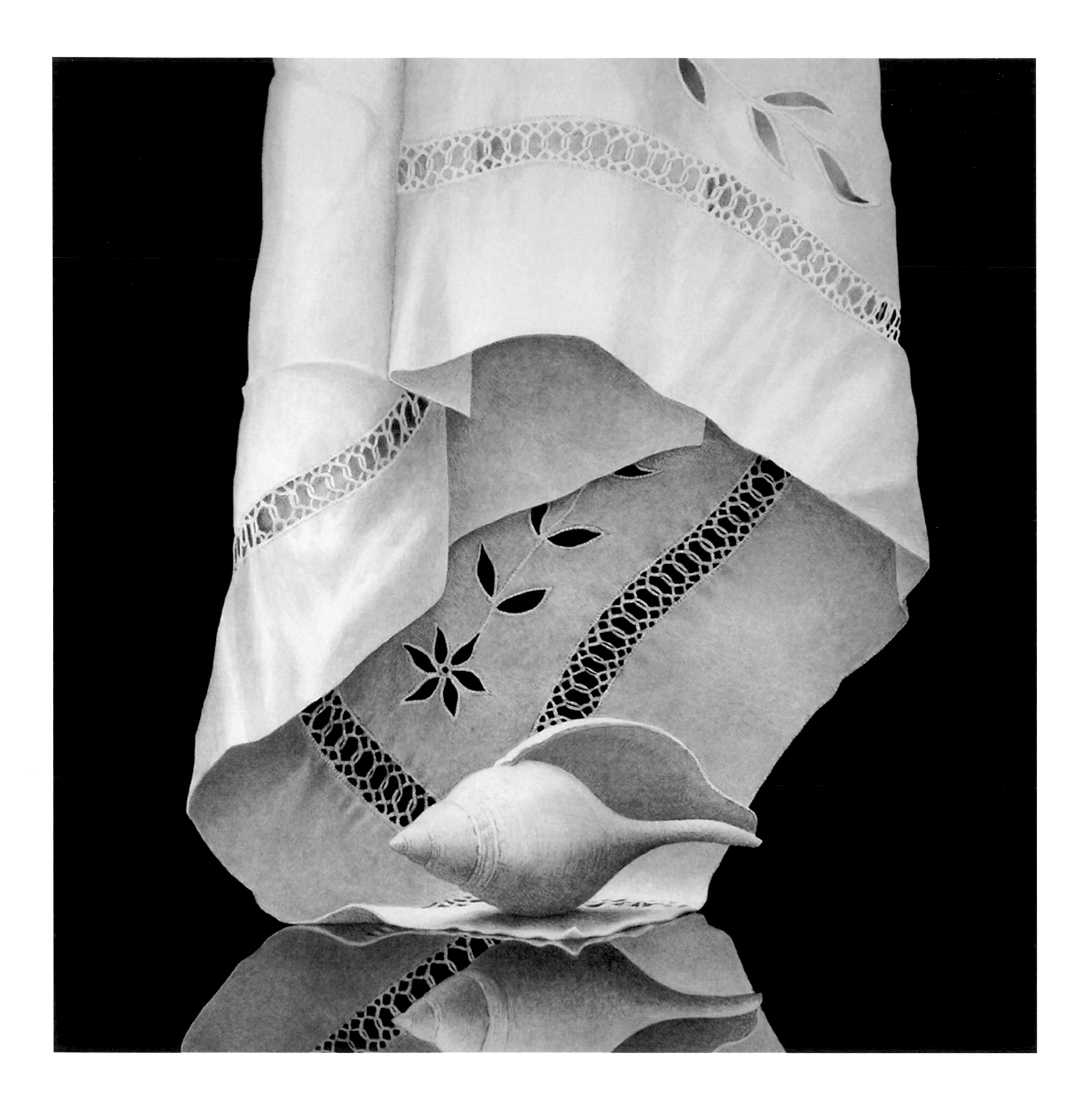

Space and Time *watercolor*
19" x 17" . 1996
Collection of the Rev. C. William Frampton, III

The weightlessness of space is not easily achieved here on planet Earth, with its gentle but pervasive gravity. I attempted to overcome this through the use of three mundane objects: a linen doily, a tulip whelk shell, and a piece of clear window glass. The reflective quality of the glass picked up the folds of the fabric, creating the illusion that the cloth and shell were floating in space.

As many of my works attest, I am fascinated with fabrics—especially ribbon and fine handmade linen and lace. Many of the woven treasures I use in my still lifes were inherited from my wife's maternal grandmother, Concetta Cammisa. She created them in Italy as part of her dowry.

Night Shade *watercolor*
26" x 19" . 1995
Collection of Dr. and Mrs. Vincent Ionata

ASCENT *watercolor*
14" x 12" . 1991
Collection of Mr. and Mrs. Lee J. Whiting

Children are natural born beachcombers and collectors, but I believe all of us, no matter our ages, yearn to explore and discover in similar ways. Our ancestors must have dreamed of setting sail to the moon centuries before it was technologically possible. When the Apollo astronauts made their lunar landing in 1969, we all felt like excited children on the shore of another world, picking up our first specimens and bringing them home for study. The painting *Ascent* represents that high-tech fulfillment of an age-old dream: brave voyagers leaving an exotic, far-off landscape with treasure in hand.

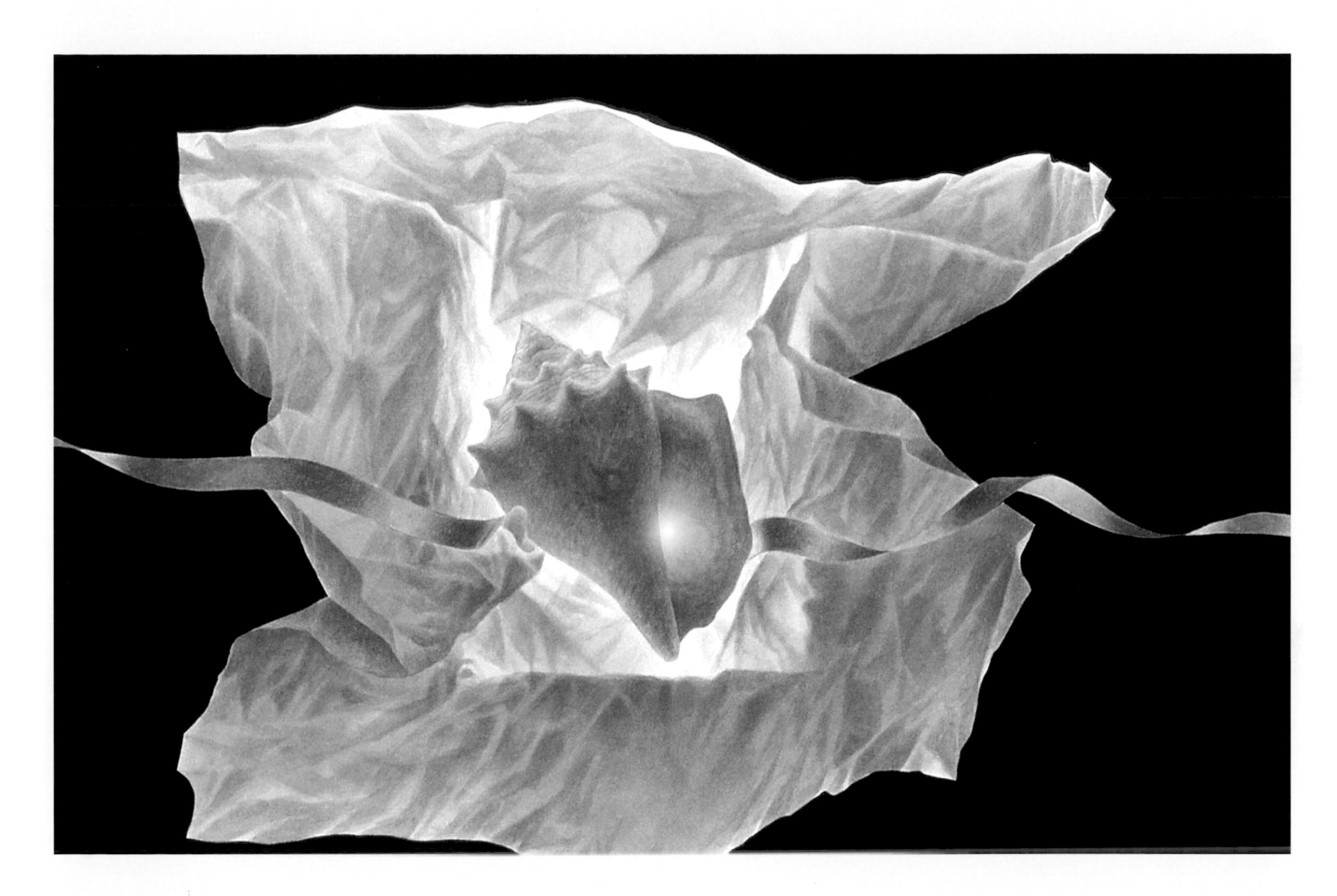

INNER LIGHT | *watercolor*
21" x 28" . 1994
Collection of David H. Hickman

Earth and Moon

watercolor
26" x 32" . 1984
Courtesy of the Smithsonian National Air and Space Museum NASA Art Collection

In the mid-1980's, having earlier taken part in the NASA Fine Arts Program, I was asked to contribute to their Planetary Collection. One of the paintings I produced for it, *Earth and Moon,* was based on the large boulder—a glacial erratic—that perches on a ledge on Mosquito Island, in Maine's Penobscot Bay (see *Island Guardian*, page 70). I had always admired the huge stone and enjoyed thinking about the history of its creation and travels. During the NASA project, my love for astronomic metaphors transformed the great stone into Earth's Moon, bound to us by history and gravity. So the painting became *Earth and Moon.*

THIN AIR *watercolor*
14" x 18" . 1992
Collection of Mr. and Mrs. Steve Masone

Architecture of the Heavens

watercolor
17.5" x 20" . 1991
Private Collection

RED PLANET BLUES

watercolor
21" x 28" . 1998
Private Collection

Blue Ribbon Stars

watercolor
19" x 33" . 2003
Private Collection

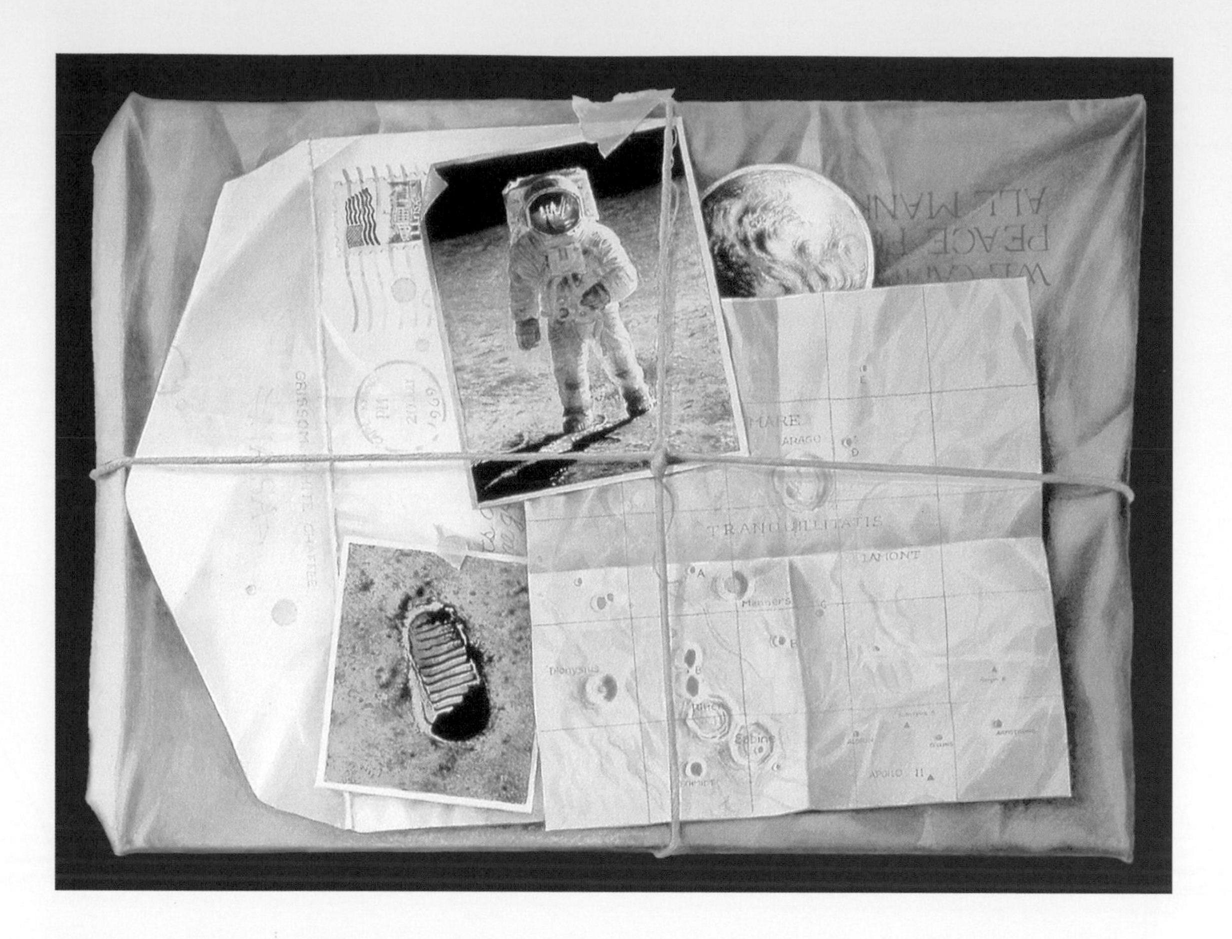

SPECIAL DELIVERY
watercolor
19" x 26" . 1999
Collection of Mr. and Mrs. Stan Friedman

MAN ON THE MOON
oil
11" x 14" . 2001
Collection of Linda L. Bean

LITTLE GARDEN PLANET

watercolor
21" x 28" . 1998
Collection of John and Alison Cooper-Mullin

On more than one occasion, I have been inspired by a songwriter's lyrics and the ideals they convey. The Canadian artist Joni Mitchell has composed many beautiful pieces with political and environmental messages. Her lyrics for the song "Ethiopia" include a masterful phrase that speaks of Earth's frailty and beauty: "Little garden planet, oasis in space." The words sparked an image in my mind of our blue planet as seen through a latticework laden with wisteria.

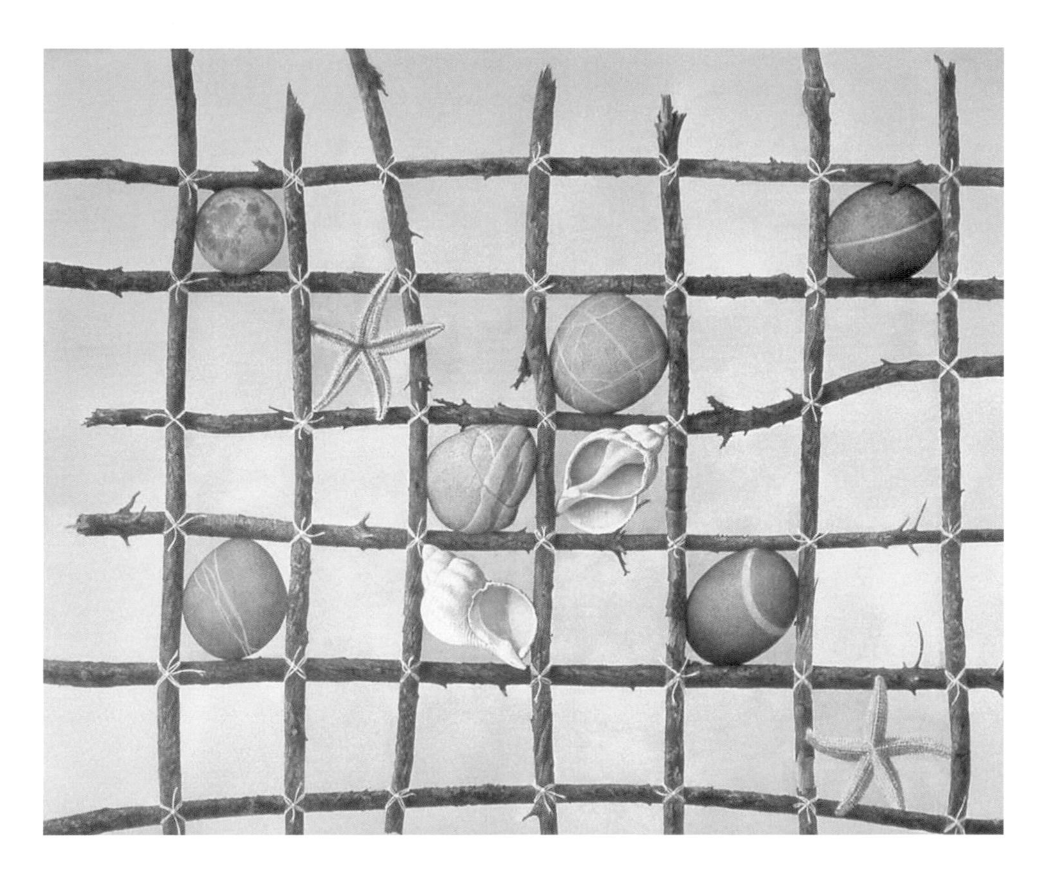

STICKS AND STONES

watercolor
26" x 33" . 1997
Private Collection

Creating a concept model for a painting allows me to study a subject at ever increasing levels of detail. There's just no substitute for having the actual artifacts in front of you. The physical contact with the objects you are manipulating adds to the emotional content of the artwork, too. The cooler temperature of a stone, the roughness of bark, the softness and flexibility of string and the tension you feel when tying it—these sensory elements transfer directly into the painting.

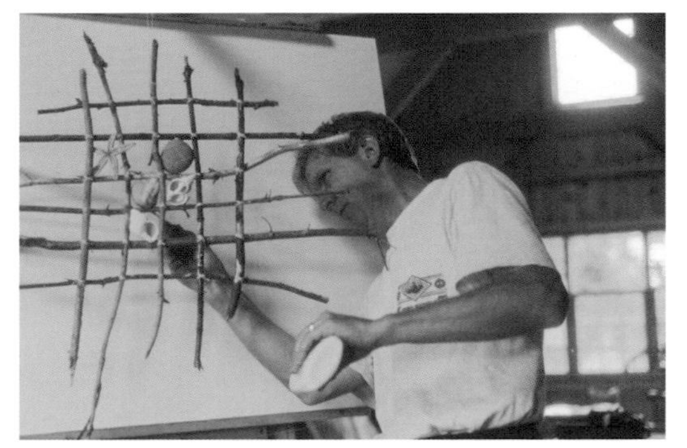

Sticks and Stones was originally prompted by my desire to create a shelf that was as naturalistic as the artifacts it held, a primitive display rack in complete harmony with its captives. At first glance, the viewer might overlook the image of our moon I placed in the upper left section of the lattice. That subtle touch plays with our sense of scale and proportion, giving the watercolor an entirely different significance.

Greg Mort constructs the still-life model for the painting Sticks and Stones.
Photograph courtesy of the Greg Mort Family Archives.

STAR FIELD — *watercolor*
21" x 28" . 1994
Private Collection

LITTLE STARS — *watercolor*
21" x 28" . 1988
Private Collection

CHAMBERS — *watercolor*
21" x 21" . 1990
Collection of Leslie Robinson

POLARIS *watercolor*
21" x 28" . 2004
Courtesy of Carla Massoni Gallery, Chestertown, Md.

Lightning on Captiva

watercolor
32" x 40" . 1979
Collection of Smithsonian American Art Museum

Just off the west coast of Florida lie the seastrand islands of Sanibel and Captiva. The latter's name allegedly traces to an infamous pirate who kept slave girls there in captivity. Today, these tropical lands are known for the abundance of seashells that blanket their beaches, offering prize specimens to the patient beachcomber.

One of the more sought-after treasures is the Lightning Whelk, named for its body-marking of jagged lines. Early one morning in 1979, I joined the rush of shell seekers and found a flawless Lightning Whelk among a vast mound of shells freshly brought in by a rough overnight tide. I knew by its vivid color and distinct markings that it couldn't have spent much time tumbling in the surf. I gathered the whelk and a pillowcase full of its neighbors to take home to my studio.

A week later, I placed this marine menagerie on a sizeable piece of plywood and tried to recreate what I had seen on the beach that morning. The Lightning Whelk was, of course, the main focus. As the weeks passed, I began to admire properties in the other, less flashy shells. They, too, had importance in the grand scheme of things.

Mechanically, the task of rendering each shell in pencil line and brush—daunting at first—came with increasing ease as I progressed. I was coming to know each shell as an individual, and moving back and forth between the still life and the watercolor paper was becoming second nature. Most surprising to me was how the different parts of the painting came together as perfectly as a jigsaw puzzle.

I hope it makes viewers feel as though they were on the beach with me that morning, finding their own *Lightning on Captiva.*

BREAKING MOON

watercolor
26" x 32" . 1994
Collection of Al and Carla Massoni

I've felt a deep love for the moon since childhood. Our family owned a small spyglass telescope, and I remember fashioning a little homemade mount so I could steady it to look skyward. The moon's image was quite small, at best, but it revealed enough detail to spur my imagination further. I also recall watching from my bedroom window as fast-moving clouds swept past a full moon. The dance of light and shadow and the wondrous rainbow effect were never less than hypnotic.

Decades later, I still love to step outside to view the night sky and drink in its deep sense of mystery. Adding another deep, dark mystery—the ocean—enhances the dramatic effect.

The Tempest | *watercolor*
32" x 40" . 1982
Private Collection

For centuries, artists have constructed models as props for their paintings as a way to control the effects of lighting and to endlessly manipulate the elements in a composition. During the mid-1980's I constructed a number of paper models of New England dories about ten inches in length for a series of watercolor paintings. For *The Tempest,* depicting a dory flung onto its side after a storm, I stranded a paper model on a handsome stone from our garden.

FIELDSTONE CASTLE

watercolor
21" x 23" . 1989
Collection of Mr. and Mrs. Doan Trevor

Under a Billion Suns

mixed media
24" x 24" . 2006
Collection of Jack and Susan Stoltz

Alchemist Art: Greg Mort

White on white and the subtle
nuance of blue satin ribbon woven
into old, finely spun lace
folded back on itself in careless layers
surrounding a box full of night sky,
stars in a distance
I can almost touch.
I can't turn past those white lights
in limitless midnight blue
now sprayed over a beach full of shells,
starfish and nautilus, clam,
and mussel, white and gray-blue
fading to green with a hint
of clay. *Stream of Stars.*
Boats: two dinghies, dry-docked, painted white
by a white barn. How many shades
of white, of an intimate clarity
of distance can this painter discern?
Golden apples in boxes of white
shadowed by white
again and the fruit is thin-
skinned Delicious, flesh warm,
as real as my hand.
A worn wooden box holds
an alchemist's treasures—
a rebus of planets and signs—a
Moon rock, an old leather book
bound in brass—Mercury's journal,
a photo of Earth from Mars, a
Phillip's head screw-
driver marked for Venus, film footage
of Saturn, the Sea God's trident and
Pluto's keys, a Jupiter space capsule
on an old stamp and Uranus
dressed as the Jack of Clubs.
The whole galaxy is scattered
on a shelf out back in the barn—
then outside the window
of a white walled-room
past the tarnished brass knob
on the open white door
of a farmhouse.
As above, so below…

—Ellen Bishop

STONE'S THROW
watercolor
22" x 18" . 1999
Collection of Terry and Christine Flynn

Cosmic Shore

watercolor
19" x 24" . 1996
Collection of Linda L. Bean

The Shining Sea

watercolor
26" x 20" . 1997
Private Collection

Fires in the Night

watercolor
21" x 27" . 1987
Private Collection

Terrestrial | *watercolor*
38" x 38" . 1997
Private Collection

Rendezvous | *acrylic*
7" x 13" . 1983
Collection of Mr. and Mrs. George D. Coffee

Nadine and I were married in 1980. *Rendezvous* celebrates that union, symbolized by two Maine dories sharing a common destination.

In my earliest Maine days, before our marriage, I often rowed alone in a small boat to Southern Island, in Tenants Harbor. Once there, I'd set up my easel and become involved in painting the lighthouse and the surrounding landscape, oblivious to all else but my work. On one particularly productive day, as the sun was sinking, I discovered that the little boat had vanished, washed out to sea.

For some time I stood on the shore, hoping a passing mariner might notice me. Finally, shouting and waving my arms wildly, I drew the attention of a lobsterman, who brought his large boat close enough to the rocks for me to jump on. (It was not the last time a waterman would come to my aid.)

Somehow the lesson I learned that day alone on Southern Island stayed with me and influenced this reassuring image for my marriage: a *pair* of small boats, off together on an adventure, but safely grounded on shore.

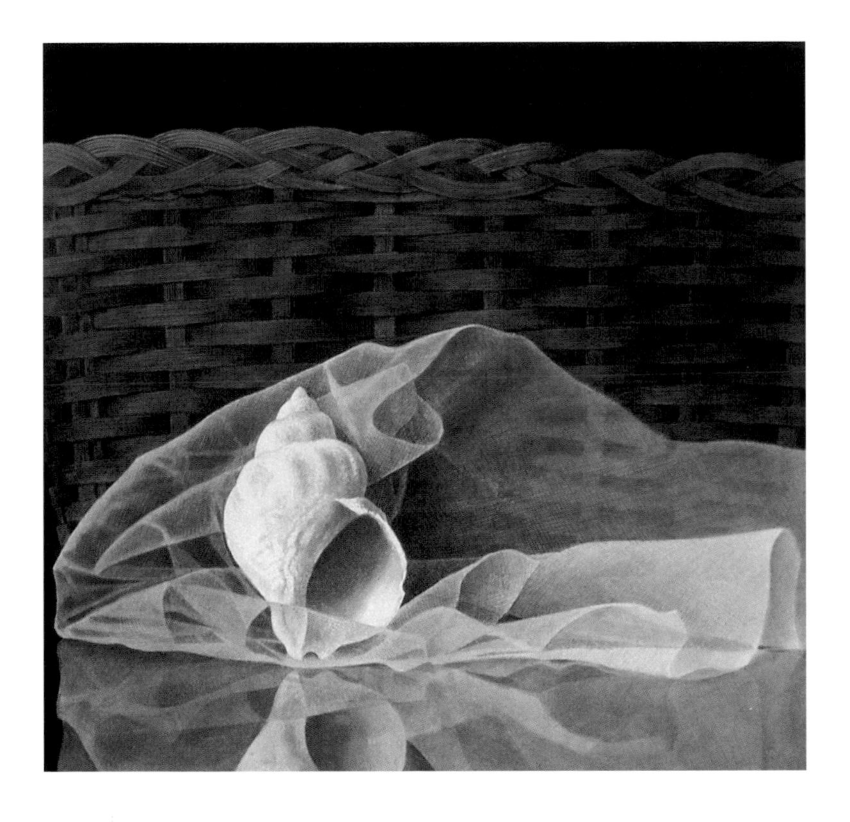

VEIL watercolor
21" x 26" . 1999
Private Collection

BROTHER AND SISTER watercolor
32" x 40" . 1983
Collection of Mr. and Mrs. Paul H. Hamlin

THE WUNDERSTRAND oil
13" x 25" . 2003
Courtesy of Somerville Manning Gallery, Greenville, De.

JUPITER AND VENUS
pastel
26" x 32" . 1999
Collection of John and Nancy Wehrle

WEATHERING
watercolor
20" x 26" . 2004
Private Collection

THE PEARL
watercolor
21" x 28" . 1993
Collection of Jonathan and Robin Plotkin

This watercolor painting was a commission for a lovely family that had given birth to a girl after three boys. The parents decided to name her Pearl. She was indeed a precious addition to their family of five. The symbolic elements in my work show her with her brothers at her side, and her parents behind the veil of stained glass. I kept the colors soft, with an emphasis on pink. And I arranged the composition so the spiral of the leaded glass makes a caring curve that points to the pearl.

TRANQUILITY
watercolor
26" x 33" . 1988
Collection of Diane L. Colgan M.D.

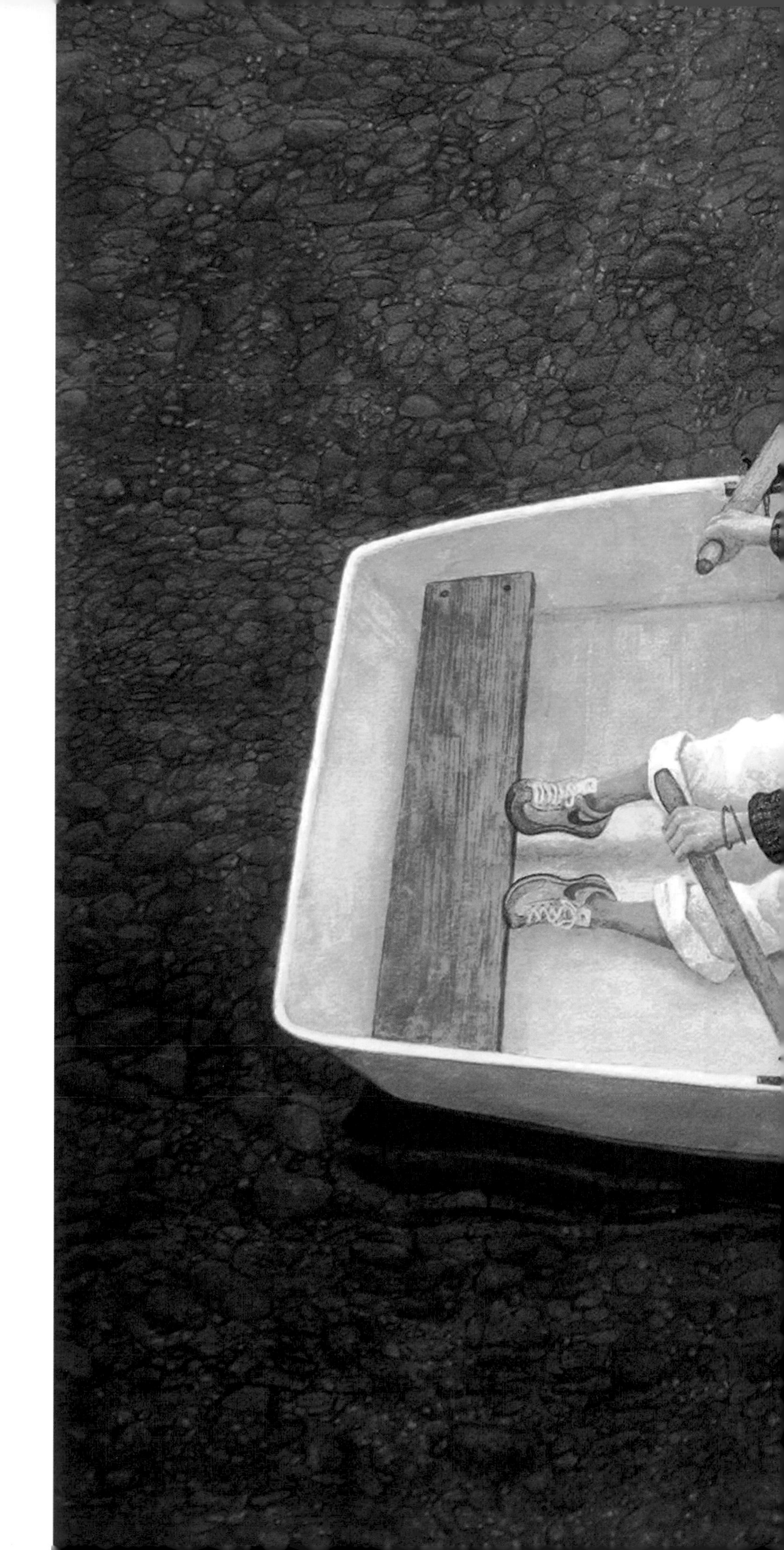

SUMMER SISTERS *watercolor*
32" x 40" . 1981
Private Collection

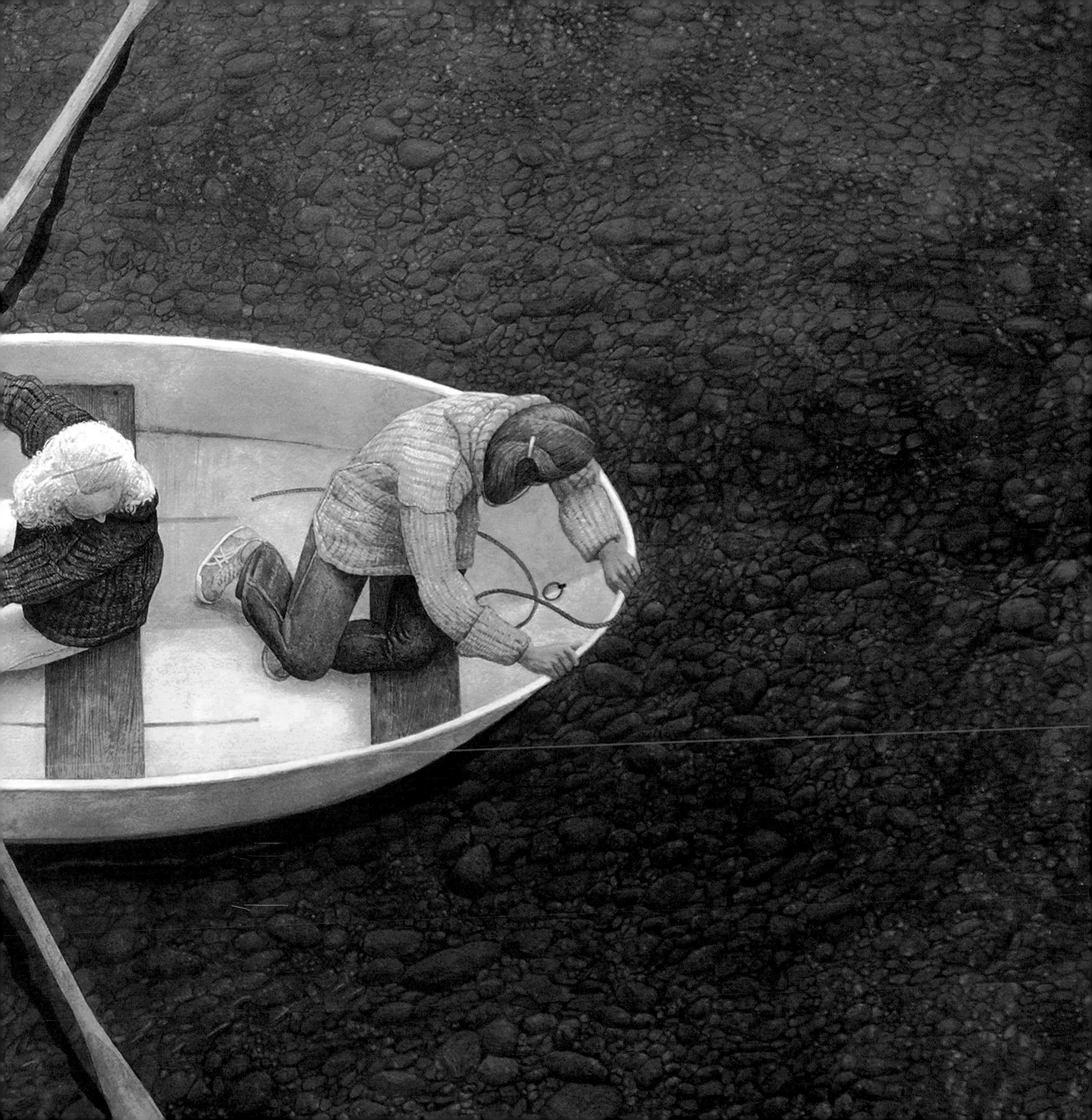

FIRST LIGHT OF DAWN

watercolor
21" x 28" . 1988
Collection of Bob and Sharon Cantor

NORTHERN COMET

watercolor
21" x 28" . 1989
Private Collection

In 1988, *Sky and Telescope* magazine was preparing a special issue that celebrated the spirit of amateur astronomers, and I was asked to create a cover image. As my thoughts gathered for this honor, I came upon the notion that the sky watcher should be presented in the most understated way, without instrumentation, not even a telescope.

For simplicity and efficiency of time, I used myself as a model. I set up two mirrors in the studio and began drawing my viewer of the night sky in a kneeling position. This pose suggested man's awareness of the Cosmos and his humble place within it. My right hand is still in contact with the mother planet in a reassuring gesture that seems to say that our ties to Earth are still strong; we aren't quite ready to stride off into the Milky Way. Conveniently, this pose also enabled me to draw while posing, as the sketchpad lay on the studio floor to my right.

INTO THE NIGHT | *watercolor*
28" x 21" . 1988
Collection of the Artist

Studio Window | *watercolor*
21" x 28" . 1988
Private Collection

My first studio at Fieldstone Castle, our home in Maine, was outfitted with an old English pub door complete with an oval leaded-glass window and a postal slot. I loved its appearance and the way it created a kind of privacy that was also welcoming. The light that came through the colored glass made the narrow sill a perfect display area for sea-born artifacts. My children and I loved to collect starfish at extra low tides, dry them out and arrange them in this place of honor.

Ring Around the Moon

watercolor
21" x 28" . 1988
Private Collection

Burnt Island

watercolor
21" x 28" . 2004
Collection of Mr. and Mrs. Edmund B. Cronin Jr.

Earthbound

watercolor
19" x 28" . 1995
Private Collection

Among my paintings that show the sky, those portraying it at night vastly outnumber daytime scenes. Since my first childhood glimpse through a telescope, I've spent thousands of hours viewing the night sky, often from my observatory in a field behind our Maryland home. Through my affiliations with two American observatories (Lowell Observatory in Arizona, and McDonald Observatory in Texas) I've been privileged to have contact with "real" astronomers, increasing my knowledge and love of the heavens.

Earthbound began with a winter outing to Triadelphia Reservoir, an impoundment on Maryland's Patuxent River surrounded by deep woods. I often go there with easel, paints, and the family spaniels to find inspiration for my landscapes. This watercolor painting combines my impressions from the reservoir and my fascination with shooting stars, or meteorites.

A prized collection of about seventy-five meteorites—bought, traded and gathered from the four corners of the Earth—are part of the clutter of my Maryland studio. Some of the most exotic of my pieces of space debris came from Mars or even further, from celestial bodies beyond our own solar system. Speckled with tiny diamonds, these latter specimens predate our own five billion years of planetary history.

Planet Maker | *mixed media*
24" x 30" . 2006
Collection of David H. Hickman

Living and traveling in Italy has left indelible impressions on me. The country's cultural influences, artistic accomplishments, scientific breakthroughs and architectural achievements stand out among the greatest in world history. Beauty is everywhere, including doorways. After returning from a trip to Pisa, I built a replica of a marvelous entrance I saw there, complete with working hinges and stucco. In *Planet Maker* it becomes the doorstep of the gods, where newly created planets are set out after completion.

MORNING STAR

mixed media
24" x 30" . 2006
Collection of Mr. and Mrs. Edmund B. Cronin Jr.

THE REALMS OF THE LARGE AND SMALL

mixed media
34" x 30" . 2006
Collection of David H. Hickman

DREAMING IN SIDEREAL TIME

watercolor
13" x 21" . 1998
Collection of Richard and Elaine Whiting

THE WATERS HERE BELOW

mixed media
24" x 24" . 2004
Courtesy of Carla Massoni Gallery, Chestertown, Md.

A childhood passes quickly when you observe it as a parent. When our son and daughter were young, I often watched them as they slept like angels, unaware of my presence and how rapidly they were moving through *my* time. This painting of my daughter Kamissa began with small, detailed drawings I made as I sat beside her bed. In the final, celebratory watercolor, *Dreaming in Sidereal Time,* it seemed fitting to adorn the pillow with stellar motifs in hopes that she would always reach for the stars.

The phrase "sidereal time" seemed apt for the title not only because it's based on measurements of the stars, but also because the sidereal day—the time it takes Earth to complete one rotation on its axis—is nearly four minutes shorter than our standard twenty-four-hour day.

Kamissa, like her brother, made it into many of my paintings awake as well as asleep. In *The Waters Here Below,* she explores a tidal pool in a surreal landscape.

BROTHERS SOJOURN

oil
32" x 60" . 2004
Collection of Mr. and Mrs. Robert Briggs

ECLIPSE — *watercolor*
12" x 12" . 1991
Private Collection

GOLD AND IRIS — *watercolor*
24" x 32" . 2006
Collection of Mr. Ronald Caplan

LEAFSCAPE — *watercolor*
21" x 28" . 2004
Collection of Mr. and Mrs. Robert Briggs

Relativistic Journey

oil
15" x 30" . 2002
Private Collection

Sometime in the far future, will we be able to transport ourselves through space and time at the speed of light? Albert Einstein believed the answer was no. He added, however, that we might reap some benefits from traveling *near* its boundary, where time itself must give way. That is, for those in rapid transit, shipboard time would pass at a snail's pace compared to the hours being lived back home.

Time Dilation, as it is called, would allow interstellar travelers to traverse immense distances without aging at the normal Earth rate. If these journeys become reality, they will probably be one-way trips; certainly none of the passengers' acquaintances would still be around upon their return; and if they stayed away long enough, neither would their home planet.

With *Relativistic Journey* I wanted to create a feeling of blinding speed; the vehicle itself has become a brilliant white light source. I chose tones that gave the composition a metallic quality. And if I could have added sound to the picture, it would have been an amazingly high pitch, almost painful to the ear.

In spite of the negatives and risks, many of us would still find ourselves inexorably drawn to the experience.

Silver Ribbon

watercolor
21" x 28" . 1995
Private Collection

Across the Sea of Space

watercolor
20" x 26" . 1986
Collection of Mr. and Mrs. Churchill Carey, Jr.

STELLAR WINDS | *watercolor*
16" x 22" . 2000
Collection of Mr. and Mrs. Robert H. Perry

There are many ways to include something of yourself in a work of art. A true self-portrait is a bit too direct for me. In the surreal work *Stellar Winds,* I chose to show only my arm extending from inside a conch shell that has appeared in many of my paintings. I hold a ribbon being unspooled in the breeze.

The idea of wind generated by the stars is a reference to the solar wind that pours out of the sun. It exerts enough pressure to propel a comet's tail at five-hundred thousand miles per hour. Futurists conjure up visions of space travel that would harness this tremendous solar force to propel large sail-like ships through the solar system at tremendous velocity. A "free ride," if you will. So *Stellar Winds* may be a prophetic work, a promise of tomorrow.

Left-Handed Time *watercolor*
26" x 30" . 1998
Collection of Foster L. Aborn and Ginger Holbrook

The beginning thoughts for a painting can flow from surprising places. In the case of *Left-Handed Time,* I first mused over the direction in which shells spiral. Most species are "Right- Handed," which means they spiral clockwise when viewed from head on. Those that curl in the opposite direction are said to be "Left-Handed." On very rare occasions, random mutation will cause a right-handed species to spiral left, and vice versa.

From there, my thoughts wandered to the direction time flows—one way, toward tomorrow. Cosmologists like to speak of a point in history when the expansion of the "Big Bang" might slow, reverse direction and become the "Big Crunch." Space-time would contract, time would flow backwards, and effects would precede causes. Such counter-intuitive notions gave birth to this painting illustrating mirrored universes, one left and one right.

WINDSWELL *watercolor*
21" x 30" . 1985
Collection of Mr. and Mrs. Howard G. Seaver

SILVER SPHERE *watercolor*
12" x 12" . 1998
Collection of Diane L. Colgan M.D.

Star Map *watercolor*
21" x 28" . 1997
Private Collection

The Fabric of Space *watercolor*
19" x 25" . 1985
Collection of the Artist

Advances in astronomy and space exploration have provided us with a window to look back in time and rewind the cosmic movie nearly to the point of Creation. These achievements have both lifted our spirits and humbled us. They also have given us a new reverence for the workings of nature. In this painting, *The Fabric of Space*, I try to draw the viewer into the Pandora's Box that holds the exciting mysteries of the cosmos.

We have, in our quest to know the unknowable, opened a doorway that will never be closed. I suppose it is a journey our ancestors embarked on countless years ago and one we will continue forever. I feel fortunate to have been alive at the moment we first ventured into the sea of space. It was my fortune, too, that Carl Sagan selected this image for his award-winning book *Pale Blue Dot*.

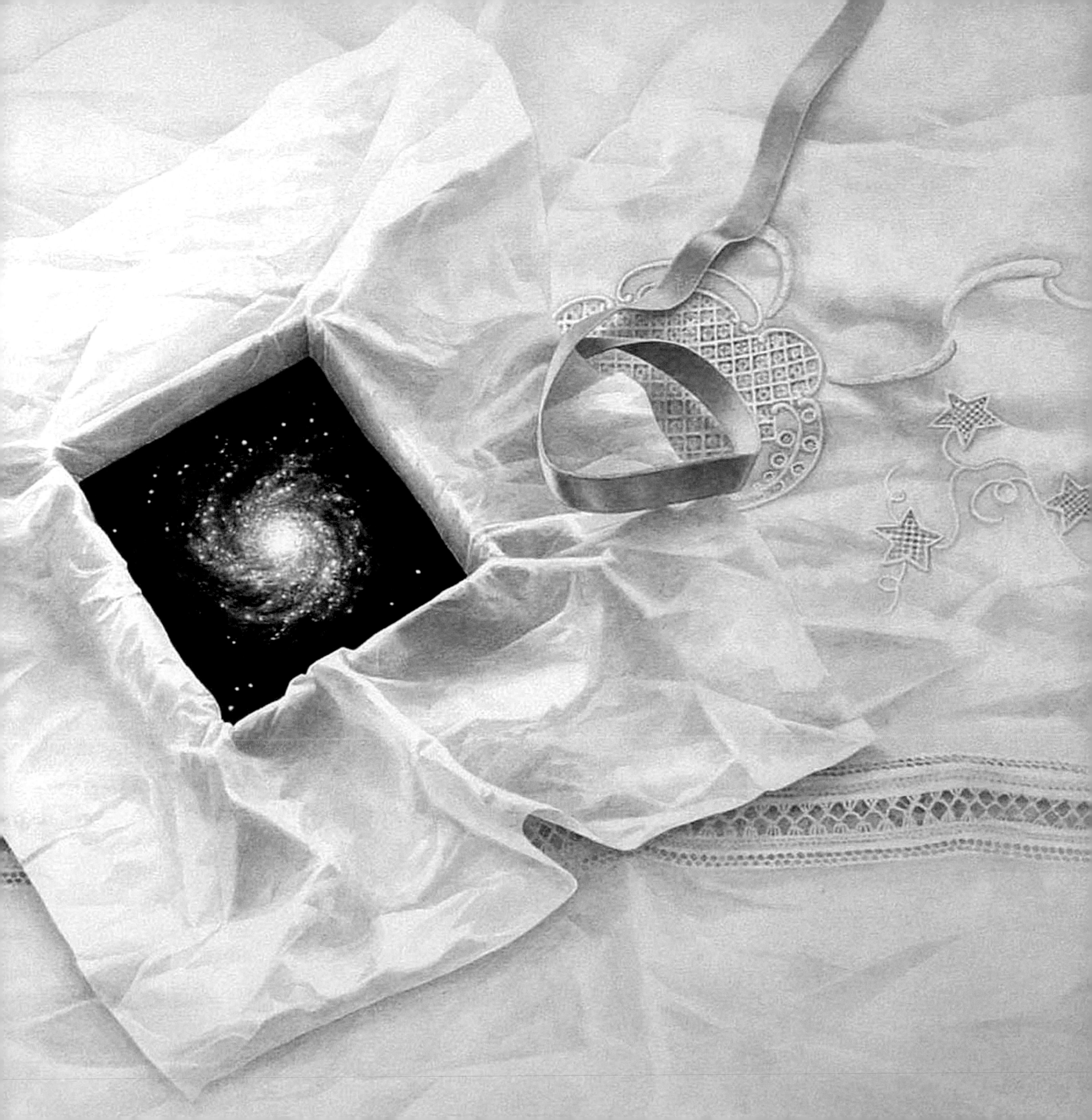

Afterword

Greg Mort's life and career have been marked by a spirit of exploration and the courage to take on new challenges. In the tradition of Leonardo da Vinci, he travels with ease between the worlds of art and science, in particular, astronomy.

From the observatory he built behind his house in Ashton, Maryland, he has observed and photographed the great celestial events of his adult life. Sometimes these celestial observations provide inspiration for paintings of imagined sky-scapes. On other occasions, as with his images of the Hale-Bopp comet, the paintings are more completely grounded in reality. Indeed, it is difficult to tell the difference between Greg's telescopic photographs of Hale-Bopp and his paintings of it.

The same acute powers of observation that Greg applies to the heavens enable him to find beauty and mystery in a pile of stones, a single shell or a forest at twilight. His meticulously executed paintings, often serene in their subdued tones, belie the restlessness suggested by his constant experimenting with new techniques. Never satisfied with his artistic status quo, he constantly stretches a medium to its limit, searching for darker darks, lighter lights, richer colors.

Greg once remarked, "The paint for all the watercolor paintings I have ever done probably could fit into a thimble." Well, maybe a couple of thimbles. In contrast to the wet-on-wet watercolors of artists such as Winslow Homer or John Singer Sargent, Greg creates his watercolors the way the old masters painted with oil: he applies layer upon layer, allowing each to dry before adding the next. This enables him to describe the visible world with realistic detail that rivals the pioneers of oil painting such as Jan van Eyck, but with the clarity of tone and color that comes only with watercolor.

When Greg began to paint in oil as well as watercolor, he already was accustomed to working in multiple layers, but he had to learn an entirely different approach. It was precisely the challenge of thinking in terms of dark to light, rather than the light-to-dark method of watercolor, that first attracted him to oil painting, a medium that enabled him to achieve deeper shadows and a wider range of tones with more subtle gradations.

No sooner had Greg mastered oil than he moved on to a new technique that combines the qualities of oil and watercolor, casein. The choice of casein, for which milk is the medium that binds the color together, was inspired by seeing the works of seventeenth-century Dutch artist Frans van Mieris, a leader of the Leiden school of *fijnschilders* (fine or finely detailed painting).

During my tenure as U.S. Ambassador to the Netherlands (1998-2001), I installed a collection of American art influenced by Dutch art and the Netherlands in the residence of the American Embassy in The Hague. Greg Mort had pride of place alongside Rembrandt Peale, Alexander Calder, and Willem de Kooning, among others. His still life *Norwood*—with motifs in the spirit of seventeenth-century Dutch still lifes, such as a lobster, starched linens and a pocket watch—adorned the cover of the catalogue of the collection. Those who looked closely could discern the names of members of the Schneider family hidden in the painting, a characteristically thoughtful, personal touch by the artist.

Greg has aptly described himself as someone who "lives his life as a creative person," pointing out that "the creative wheels are always turning, not just when you sit down to do a painting." Throughout his career, he has stimulated his creative energy through an astonishing array of activities that include painting, drawing, printmaking, crafting models, and building and using telescopes. His voyage of discovery continues, and we are the lucky witnesses.

Cynthia P. Schneider, PhD
Distinguished Professor in the Practice of Diplomacy
Georgetown University

NORWOOD *watercolor*
21" x 28" . 1998
Collection of Dr. Thomas J. and Ambassador Cynthia P. Schneider

A Conversation with the Artist

Throughout his life Greg Mort has combined his two great passions: art, and exploring the wonders of the universe. Individually and together, the microcosms and macrocosms of nature play roles in classic Greg Mort images. In an interview with **J. Kelly Beatty**, Editor of *Night Sky* magazine and Executive Editor of *Sky & Telescope,* the artist shares insights into the experiences and philosophies that inform his work.

Q: Greg, the mysteries of the universe have captured and been reflected in the artistic imagination since the dawn of man. This seems like a natural venue for you. How and when did this fascination first develop in your artwork?

Exploring the wonders of nature, and especially the night sky, started about the same time as did my fascination with art. When I was 13 years old, a friend invited me to have a look through his telescope. It was a very basic instrument, a cardboard tube and small mirror of low quality. Nonetheless, the view of the first-quarter Moon was mind-boggling. You could actually see craters and mountains on another world. I was electrified, and that feeling has never left. Forty years later I find myself returning to telescopes with that same sense of wonder.

All this began the same time as the Apollo Moon missions. Everyone was bitten by the space bug; it was contagious. By the time I began my career as a professional artist in the late 1970's, Carl Sagan had released his award-winning science series *Cosmos.* This further stimulated the development of astronomical elements in my work. *Cosmos* was a feast visually as well as intellectually.

I began to acquire a number of more substantial telescopic instruments. Little by little, themes of space science entered my paintings—obvious or subtle, but steadily more dominant. Then in 1983, I attended an exhibit at the National Air and Space Museum called "The Artist and the Space Shuttle." It was an amazing collection of artistic renditions of what was then a young shuttle program. I contacted the NASA program director and sent in examples of my work. To my delight I was accepted and assigned to cover Space Shuttle Flight 7 with America's first female astronaut, Sally Ride. This was another experience that helped forge the art-science union.

Q: Like Whistler, Remington and Turner, you frequently depict nocturnal scenes. Do you feel these artists have influenced your artwork? And how is your work different?

Paintings of and about the night are a rarity when compared to those done in the light of day. My love for the night has certainly been enhanced by my endless hours at the telescope under the heavens. These hours have also increased my appreciation for the subtle qualities of the night sky. The artists you mentioned are well known for their nocturnal work, and without question one creative spirit will impress and stimulate another.

My paintings are similar to theirs in the way they celebrate the natural wonder of the night. But mine have a more direct link to science and astronomy. An example of this is the watercolor *Golden Spiral* [page 15]. It conveys two important themes. One is the beauty of nature in the realms of the large and small, your macro and micro. The other is the mathematical harmony represented by the Fibonacci sequence of numbers; it was developed by the Italian mathematician who helped introduce the Hindu-Arabic numerical system into Western Europe a millennium ago.

Q: Your still lifes and landscapes often have astronomical references and/or hidden images or scientific messages. Do you do this for your own pleasure, or are you seeking to engage the viewer on some other level?

The answer is, both. I do it for myself as a means of reverent celebration, but I also want to convey this appreciation to others. Art is, in the end, a way to communicate. I hold the workings of nature in such high esteem that I am compelled to pay homage time and time again, never growing weary of interpreting my fascination.

Q: Your paintings, especially your images with celestial underpinnings, are quite thought-provoking. Are you actively attempting to stimulate inquiry?

Have you ever felt the wonderful tingling on the back of the neck that comes with discovery? That feeling of excitement, an almost euphoric one, is one of the loftiest sensations we can experience. That is what I'm after in these works. If only for a moment the viewer can have that sense of something grand, then the work has real meaning and achieves a real purpose.

Q: In your paintings *Oceans* and *Stream of Stars* you combine the celestial and the terrestrial landscapes with great impact.

Both paintings are expressions of extreme scales. In *Stream of Stars* [page 9] we are confronted by the immenseness of the sky that lies beyond our immediate horizon. As we view the universe from the perspective of a lowly snail, we're reminded of our beginnings and of our personal voyage from the tidal pools in ancient oceans. Seeing these extremes, perhaps we ask: How far have we come? How far will we go? What is our destiny in the far-flung future? So much of what I strive for in my work is about this voyage of discovery.

Oceans [front cover] is also an anthem to this journey. Here we again see the shore strewn with treasures from the sea. But if viewers look closely, they can pick out a tiny Earth and Moon in the sand and see planets in the foam and water—worlds adrift in space and time.

Q: You are frequently referred to as an artist/astronomer because you move between both worlds. How have you been able to combine your vocation and avocation so successfully?

One of the delights of being an artist is the opportunity to enter into partnerships with other professions. Art provides a bridge that spans many rivers. Science throughout history has had a connection with art, one discipline enhancing the other. Leonardo DaVinci is perhaps the most famous example. Art and science share similarities in methods of observation, data collection, and an appreciation for the way things are put together. Astronomy, one of the most beautiful of the sciences, has long relied on the interpretive powers and expressive nature of artistic renderings, and still does. It has been my good fortune to have affiliations with two major American astronomical institutions. I was commissioned by the University of Texas' McDonald Observatory to document the construction of their largest telescope via a series of charcoal drawings. In partnership with the Lowell Observatory in Flagstaff, Arizona, I have been involved with projects that include sculpture and a large-scale centennial mural.

Q: Your works are strikingly contemporary. Who are your mentors?

I've always believed that creative individuals, whatever the medium, should provide insights into their particular time in history. I would hope that future art historians could look at my paintings and know straight away that they were a product of this time period—the dawn of our venture out into the sea of space. In earlier eras artists often accompanied expeditions to new worlds from pole to pole and everywhere in between. The Luminist artists William Bradford, Albert Bierstadt, Thomas Cole, and Frederic Church depicted the grandeur of nature in some of these newly explored lands. I follow in their footsteps, in my own way.

Q: A common question for artists is whether they dream in color or black and white. Taking it a step further, do you think in terms of day or night?

I joke that night is my favorite time of day. What I really mean is that in the back of my mind I have a night awareness. When you have a love for things astronomical, a part of your brain keeps a little running log of the positions of the visible planets, the phases of the Moon and, importantly, will it be clear tonight? With this awareness always present, it's no surprise that my works include so many night images.

Q: Why do you think Carl Sagan featured your paintings *Stewardship* [page 56] and *Fabric of Space* [page 135] in his book *Pale Blue Dot*?

As I mentioned, Carl Sagan had a great impact on me with his powerful *Cosmos* series. It was a special thrill to have my paintings in one of his last books. In a letter, he wrote that the images "resonated well" with chapters titled "A Universe Not Made for Us" and "Exploring Other Worlds and Protecting This One".

Q: There is often a feeling of a *double entendre* in the titles for your paintings. One that comes to mind is *Earthbound*, which shows a wonderful meteor in flight over a river landscape. I sense that the object in flight is earthbound, but also that we ourselves are bound to the Earth. Are titles and images like this meant to have multiple meanings?

I can spend hours or even days thinking about titles. What you picked up on here was not part of my plan. Nonetheless it illustrates perfectly how much the viewers of art bring to the table, how they add life to a piece in ways not imagined by the artist. Painting is a means of communication—a performance, if you will—that works in both directions. An artistic voyage without a destination—the viewer—would have little meaning and would lead nowhere. ❖

MUSEUM COLLECTIONS

Smithsonian American Art Museum, Washington, D.C.
Smithsonian National Air and Space Museum, Washington, D.C.
Delaware Art Museum, Delaware
Corcoran Gallery of Art, Washington, D.C.
Portland Museum of Art, Maine
Brandywine River Museum, Pennsylvania
The Academy Art Museum of Easton, Maryland
University of Padova, Padova, Italy
Farnsworth Art Museum, Maine
Sun Cities Museum of Art, Arizona
Mesa Southwest Museum, Arizona
Montgomery County Public Art Collection, Maryland
City of Boston Fine Arts Collection, Massachusetts
Parkersburg Art Center, West Virginia
Sandy Spring Museum, Maryland
Smithsonian's NASA Art Collection, Washington, D.C.
Maryland Artists Collection, University of Maryland, University College, Maryland
National Astronomy and Ionosphere Center at Cornell University, New York
Lowell Observatory, Arizona
McDonald Observatory, Texas
Vatican Observatory, Rome, Italy
NASA Goddard Space Flight Center, Maryland
Wriston Art Center, Lawrence University, Wisconsin

SELECTED SOLO MUSEUM EXHIBITIONS AND INTERNATIONAL SHOWS

2006 Grand Hotel National, Lucerne, "Greg Mort – Natural Wonders"
2005 North Museum, "Nightwatch" Traveling Exhibition
2004 Sandy Spring Museum, "Nightwatch"
1999 Academy Art Museum of Easton, "Visual Memory"
1997 Sandy Spring Museum, "Appleworks"
1994 Springfield Art Museum, "Inspirations"
Galleria Prova, Tokyo, Japan, "Greg Mort,"
1992 Parkersburg Art Center, "Inspirations"
Grand National Hotel, Lucerne, "Greg Mort"
1991 Sun Cities Museum of Art, "Greg Mort Watercolors"
1988 Maryland Science Center, "The Art of Greg Mort"
1986 Space Telescope Institute, "Greg Mort Watercolors"
1981 Singer Museum, Laren, Netherlands, "Greg Mort Watercolors"

SELECTED GROUP EXHIBITIONS

Continuing:
Smithsonian National Air and Space Museum, "Exploring the Planets" Collection
Artrain USA, "Artistry of Space"
Smithsonian National Air and Space Museum, "Generous Friends: Building an Art Collection for the Smithsonian"
Smithsonian Traveling Art Collection Exhibitions, "Visions of Flight, the Artist and the Space Shuttle"
McDonald Observatory, "Building the Hobby-Eberly Telescope"
Lowell Observatory, "A Century of Discovery"
2002 Lighthouse Museum (Key West), "Visions of Realism"
2001 Wayne Art Center (Pa.) "Meditations on Small Objects"
The White House, National Historic Trust, "Saving America's Treasures"
1993 Delaware Art Museum, "The Private Eye"
The Portland Museum of Art, "Solstice"
Brandywine River Museum, "Twenty-Fifth Anniversary"
Sun Cities Museum of Art, "Space Fantasies – Space Realities"
1991 Smithsonian National Air and Space Museum, "Art of the Cosmic Age"
Parkersburg Art Center, "American Realism '91"
Smithsonian National Air and Space Museum, "Space Shuttle Art"
1989 International Association of Astronomical Artists, "Dialogues," touring exhibition to Moscow, Minsk, and Kiev
Parkersburg Art Center, "American Realism '89"
1988 Smithsonian American Art Museum, "Close Focus"
1987 Academy Art Museum of Easton, "Fowl Orientation"
1986 Smithsonian National Air and Space Museum, "Looking at Earth"
Corcoran Gallery of Art, "Benefit Gala"
Farnsworth Art Museum, "Artist Greetings"
1985 Smithsonian National Air and Space Museum, "Fire and Ice"
Corcoran Gallery of Art, "Benefit Gala"
1984 Portland Museum of Art, "Maine Drawing Biennial"
Farnsworth Art Museum, "Maine Art Today"
1971 Munson-Williams-Proctor Arts Institute, New York, "34th Annual Exhibition, Artists of Central New York"

SELECTED HONORS, AWARDS AND COMMISSIONS

2004 Lowell Observatory Bronze Sculpture Commission
1999 Carl Sagan Award Design Commission
1990 Parkersburg Art Center American Realism Purchase Award
1989 Parkersburg Art Center American Realism Purchase Award
1986 Corcoran Gallery of Art, "Best in Show"
1986 Smithsonian National Air and Space Museum, "Looking at Earth," Second Grand Prize
1985 Corcoran Gallery of Art, "Best in Show"

Milestones

1952 Born in Syracuse, New York, the second of two sons to a Georgia-raised mother and a father of Finnish descent; recognized early on for his artistic talents.

1971 Munson-Williams-Proctor Arts Institute in Utica, New York, features Mort's first museum exhibition.

1977 Summer journey to Maine, which he (and later his family) will continue annually.

1979 The Smithsonian American Art Museum acquires *Lightning on Captiva* for permanent collection. Featured in "Close Focus" exhibition.

1980 Marries Nadine Masone; they settle home and studio in rural Ashton, Maryland.

1981 First international exhibition, at the Singer Museum, the Netherlands. Shows follow in Japan, Switzerland, Italy and Russia.

1983 Commissioned as NASA artist producing a body of ten works for Smithsonian Institution museums.

1884 Kamissa and Jonathan, twin inspirations, are born.

1985 Begins association with Somerville Manning Gallery, Greenville, Delaware.

1985 *Year of the Comet* acquired by Smithsonian's National Air and Space Museum for the Hall of Planets. Featured in "Fire and Ice" exhibition.

1986 Corcoran Gallery of Art awards Best-in-Show honors for *Dreams* and acquires it for the Gallery's permanent collection.

1987–1995 Associated with Franz Bader Gallery, Washington, D.C.

1988 Morts restore historic Fieldstone Castle, former home of artist and astronomer Russell Porter in Port Clyde, Maine, as summer home and studio.

1992 Begins association with Carla Massoni Gallery, Chestertown, Maryland.

1993 President and Mrs. Clinton acquire *Stewardship* and display it in the White House.

1994 Creates first public art commission, the mural *Century of Discovery*, for Lowell Observatory 100th anniversary celebration.

1994 Carl Sagan's book Pale Blue Dot features Mort watercolors *Stewardship* and *Fabric of Space*.

1995–96 Residing in Montepulciano, Italy, completes special commission for University of Padua and Vatican: *The Three Galileos*.

1998 Commissioned to create Carl Sagan Award and official Sagan portrait for the Smithsonian National Air and Space Museum's Steven F. Udvar–Hazy Center.

2006 North Museum in Lancaster, Pennsylvania, opens traveling exhibition "Nightwatch ~ Greg Mort," which then tours the country.

2007 Academy Art Museum in Easton, Maryland, receives promised gift of single largest collection of Greg Mort paintings, more than 25 watercolors and oils.

Index of Paintings